PRESUPPOSITION AND TRANSCENDENTAL INFERENCE

Presupposition & Transcendental Inference

Humphrey Palmer

> 'There must be such things as witches, since there are laws against witches, and it is not conceivable that laws should be made against that which does not exist'
>
> Chief Justice Hale, 1676

ST. MARTIN'S PRESS
New York

© 1985 Humphrey Palmer
All rights reserved. For information write:
St. Martin's Press, Inc., 175 Fifth Avenue, New York, NY 10010
Printed in Great Britain
First published in the United States of America in 1985

Library of Congress Cataloging in Publication Data

Palmer, Humphrey.
   Presupposition and transcendental inference.

   Bibliography: p.
   Includes index.
   1. Presupposition (Logic) 2. Transcendental logic.
3. Inference (Logic) 4. Knowledge, Theory of.
I. Title.
BC199.P73P35   1985   160   84-18384
ISBN 0-312-64173-7

CONTENTS

Acknowledgements
Analysis of chapters

Introduction		1
I	Is scepticism sensible?	3
II	The Cogito	16
III	What the Cogito refutes	27
IV	Presupposition and backward argument	38
V	Kant's vindication of geometry	50
VI	Our world	70
VII	How presupposition works	84
VIII	Backward moves in current debate	106
IX	Metaphysical research	117
X	Arguing transcendentally	137
XI	Changing spectacles	158
Bibliography		180
Index		207

to

ELIZABETH

ACKNOWLEDGEMENTS

Collingwood started me on this topic, some twenty years ago. Many others have helped me since, among them Messrs J. A. Brunton, G. Buchdahl, P.Balasubramanian, V.Deshpande, D.Emmet, D.M.Evans, A.P.Griffiths, K.L.Ketner, O.Leaman, K.Shah, T.Smiley, R.S.Woolhouse; and the members of seminars at Cardiff, Gregynog, Dharwar, Bombay, Shillong and Tambaram; and, of course, the writers of many books and articles. With so many guides I perhaps ought not to claim all the remaining errors as my own; but I would still like readers to tell me what and where they are.

I have been much helped, in writing the book, by a Visiting Scholarship at Corpus Christi College, Cambridge, and by three terms of study leave. One of these was spent in part at the Dr.S.Radhakrishnan Institute of Advanced Study at the University of Madras, with assistance from the British Council.

Some debts to earlier writers are indicated in the Bibliography. Not mentioned there, but presupposed, is the ready help of many librarians, seen and unseen, in Cardiff, Cambridge, Oxford and Madras, and elsewhere through Inter-Library Loan.

Several earlier writings of mine made their contribution to this book, and I now thank again the editors and publishers. Particular reference should be made to the items in <u>Ratio</u>, <u>International Logic Review</u> and <u>Kantstudien</u>, which are developed further in chapters I - III and V - VI.

I had valued and patient help with typing from Shirley Wollen, Jean Barber, Margaret Leishman, Jill Palmer and K.P.Achuthan. Richard Stoneman gave helpful advice on the editing. Diane Walker, of the college Computing Centre, introduced me to a SuperBrain, by which the final copy for printing was produced.

I am grateful for all their encouragement.

University College, Humphrey Palmer
Cardiff

ANALYSIS OF CHAPTERS

I IS SCEPTICISM SENSIBLE?

1 Descartes proposed doubting everything, experimentally; 2 though not so as to believe the opposite. 3 We can't disbelieve X on purpose, but we can decide not to rely on it. 4 Peirce's objection that such doubt is unreal seems dubious. 5 Wittgenstein's claim that doubt presumes some prior beliefs is correct, but does not touch Descartes, 6 who turned 'sceptic' only to see how much we really knew.

II THE COGITO

7 This formula did express an inference, 8 which assumes that actions need agents, so cannot prove this point. 9 The first-person 'I' makes the premiss less deniable, but emptier. 10 Reflective self-knowledge is still available, as before.

III WHAT THE COGITO REFUTES

11 Presumptive circularity described. 12 Inconsistent triads do yield refutations which are not p-circular. 13 Descartes' Cogito was not just a 'performatory certitude'(Hintikka). 14 Why such 'self-verifying' statements, if made, are undeniable.

Note A. Are Syllogisms circular?

IV PRESUPPOSITION AND BACKWARD ARGUMENT

15 Statements need subjects, to refer to. 16 Arguing 'back' from the statement to its subject is p-circular, 17 and linguistic in effect, a Humpty-Dumpty argument. 18 Review of ways to deal with doubt.

Note B. Ad hominem arguments.

V   KANT'S VINDICATION OF GEOMETRY

19 Elements contributed by us 20 should at least be well-known to us. 21 Geometrical construction as 'reading-in', 22 put forward as the only way to a deductive universal science of Space. 23 This backward argument is essential to <u>Critique</u> as well as <u>Prolegomena</u>. 24 Survey of sets of views shown inconsistent by this line of reasoning.

                        Note C. Kant's sciences of Time.

VI   OUR WORLD

25 The debating position is different in physics, where some concepts are already regarded as contributed. 26 But do they 'fit'? 27 "Well, they work". 28 And physicists cannot manage otherwise. 29 Does this argument work "back"? 30 Kant's proof that I need Things, as clocks. 31 Review of his p-circular arguments.

VII   HOW PRESUPPOSITION WORKS

32 Referential presupposition is irreflexive, anti-symmetrical and 'ganderous', unlike implication. It is directional and non-functional. 33 As propriety is confirmed by verifying presuppositions, reasoning back from it to them is circular. This is so even for a functional analogue ('posing'). 34 The relation of a complex concept to its elements is closely similar, 35 showing a sort of system and priority, 36 on which inferences can be based. 37 The relation of an argument to a missing premiss is quite similar. 38 What is taken for granted may not be recognized, and may be important, and may be wrong.

                  Note D. What linguists do with 'presuppose'.

VIII BACKWARD MOVES IN CURRENT DEBATE

39 Presupposes, not implies: (a) impossible duties; (b) infallible knowledge; (c) counting and comparing things. 40 'As is' or 'as described'? (a) what appears (Kant); (b) looking for Nessie (Otto); (c) theory-laden terms. 41 Bricks and straw: (a) too good to be true; (b) branch-cutting; (c) not in front of the children (Thrasymachus).

IX METAPHYSICAL RESEARCH

42 Which comes first? (a) metaphysical priority (Locke); (b) too much hangs thereby. 43 Refuting reductions: (a) People are not disposable; (b) knowledge is not, but requires truth (Butler); (c) what bodies are made of (Hume); (d) conceptual nit-picking (Bradley); (e) robots keep out (Malcolm). 44 Descriptive metaphysics: (a) it's got to be stopped (Denning); (b) indispensable individuals (Strawson); (c) what just must be there (Harrison); (d) ultimate moral principles (Griffiths).

X TRANSCENDENTAL INFERENCE

45 Kant's usage of the term. 46 His remarks on transcendental proof. 47 Our classification of arguments by that name. 48 The arguments are ordinary, but the premisses are unobtainable. 49 Concluding challenge on transcendental proof.

Note E. How Kant may have come by the term.

XI CHANGING SPECTACLES

50 The failure of transcendental argument leaves us back at our 'sceptical' starting-point. 51 Pragmatic and transcendental attempts at justifying principles. 52 Collingwood's scheme of Absolute Presuppositions, revised. 53 Existential assumptions differ from methodical postulates. 54 Principles do not determine thought. 55 The Work of Definition, tidying up our conceptual scheme. 56 Reasons for basic, systematic change. 57 Transcendental arguments may help to show which presuppositions are ultimate, within a scheme. 58 Principles and paradigms.

REFERENCES

Books are cited by author and page-number, articles by author and date.

'cp' suggests broad agreement, or more detail.
'cf' an alternative or opposing view.
'f' means 'and the following page(s)'.
'#' precedes the number of a section.
Cross-references are to <u>sections</u> of this book.

Most quotations from Kant are translated afresh, with reference to

A Critique of Pure Reason, 1781
P Prolegomena to any future Metaphysic ..., 1783
B Critique, second edition, 1787.

For the citations from Descartes, page-numbers of the edition by Haldane and Ross are given in the Bibliography; and similar provision is made for quotations from Peirce.

INTRODUCTION

This book is about presupposition, a relation more relied upon than understood, and one which figures in some famous arguments:

Thoughts need thinkers.
Unless people had property, nobody could suffer damages.
Principles can't be innate unless ideas are too.
Only dirty people wash.
All the change and process in this world point back to some original Initiative.

These arguments work 'back' from some given present fact to some other, presupposed by it, and claim that other must have been so first: since otherwise we could never have been 'given' that 'fact' from which our argument began:

This moves. That moves ... but motion requires a mover (in our experience) to set it off. So someone must have started all of it, or all those movements we noticed could never have begun.

Many such backward arguments from presupposition turn out to suffer from 'presumptive circularity', an insidious and debilitating fallacy not noted in the logic-books; which boils down to this, that the conclusion of the argument would need to be known in advance, for the purpose of establishing the premisses!

Introduction

Now our question is: do all the arguments called transcendental run backward, and commit this fallacy? And where does that leave us, if the proof they offered is unusable?

It may be helpful to sketch out now the route we propose to take in tackling these questions:

First, we explain what sorts of sceptical doubt philosophers have been most anxious to rebut in deploying transcendental arguments. Then we explain how such arguments are supposed to work and what our objection to them is. The example used, for both purposes, is the metaphysics of Descartes: the familiar instance serving to introduce twists and turns and terminology that may be unfamiliar. These introductions occupy chapters One to Three.

In chapter Four we expound the notion of presupposition, and show why arguments 'back' from a presupposition to the item presupposed will normally suffer from presumptive circularity. In chapters Five and Six this critique is applied to Kant's central and 'transcendental' arguments.

The properties and varieties of presupposition are considered further in chapter Seven. Chapters Eight and Nine illustrate its use and abuse in inference, by an array of current slogans and arguments which turn on this relationship.

Chapter Ten then presents in summary form our findings regarding transcendental arguments, what they are and what they can and cannot do.

Scepticism, we conclude, cannot be shown false by transcendental arguments, as that would make them circular. But it may be made untenable. How then should we regard those fundamental principles which the transcendental analyst fails to establish but whose contraries the sceptic cannot coherently enunciate? A final chapter will seek Collingwood's help in placing these unprovable-yet-undeniable starting-points of all our thought and inference.

Chapter One

IS SCEPTICISM SENSIBLE?

There is an old and honoured line of argument, impressive in presentation but of uncertain force, for refuting sceptics with. This defence against intellectual banditry was first erected by Descartes and later squared up in proper masonry by Kant; and is now available in portable concrete units, prefabricated to customers' requirements under the brand name of Transcendental Arguments.

We are to enquire how such defences are supposed to work, and what they actually prove; but first we must see what sort of attack they are intended to repulse. What is this scepticism, which transcendental arguers will defend us all against?

There are, of course, sceptics and sceptics: as there are various things one might be dubious about, and several possible purposes in doubting them. Descartes' main concern was with doubts that affected Science:- Was observation generally reliable? Could mathematics be mistaken? Might memories be deceptive and everything a dream? We have to consider if such very general doubts mean anything, and what he had in mind when raising them, in order to see just what he might hope to achieve by his version of The Argument.

1. EXPERIMENTAL DISBELIEF

Why not begin your thinking life again, by doubting everything? Childhood and education have left you too well padded with belief. You'll have to cut down. Intellectual fitness demands that you make a habit of believing less. A complete fast may be best to begin with: believe nothing at all for a while. Try treating everything you ever heard as false.

At once the objection is heard: you can't doubt everything at once. To doubt <u>this</u>, you must be sure of <u>that</u>. Some truths must be known, and admitted as such, or we shall have no standards by which other items could be reckoned dubious. A general scepticism will defeat itself. And as Descartes proposed to start with an entirely general doubt, we need not follow him beyond this point.

This objection does not touch Descartes, for the doubts he proposed raising were neither permanent nor entirely general. He just wanted to try it on, for once; to see what could be doubted if he gave his mind to it. Some opinions, surely, would be found undoubtable. Which these are, he hopes to discover by trying to doubt everything in turn, deliberately, experimentally.

But surely there won't be much left if we insist on doubting everything we can? Our indubitables form a meagre collection, insufficient for ordinary life or even for a sceptical philosopher, so the attempt to discard all discardables will defeat itself. Maybe so; but Descartes did not propose to discard whatever turned out disbelievable. Instead he meant to select for special treatment those items which turned out undisbelievable. After turning out all the apples in the basket, lest the bad infect the good, he picks them over and puts the good ones back again (<u>Replies</u> 7). He is busy shaking things, to see which ones are shakeable, "that those things which cannot be shaken may remain".

2. BELIEVING DIFFERENT

Sometimes in matters of behaviour one has to follow questionable views as though they were beyond doubt. But in theoretical questions it is just the other way about: here everything which can be thought at all dubious must be rejected as if it were completely wrong, so as to see if any beliefs are left which are indubitable (Discourse 4).

Gassendi favoured the programme of "stripping off every prejudged opinion". But why not just say so, i.e. indicate which beliefs seem unreliable, then pick out those which stand as true? "For treating them all as false is not discarding preconceived ideas but trading them for another lot" (Objections 5).

This objection takes 'treat as false' to mean 'consider to be untrue': and surely treating-X-as-false will mean taking not-X to be true? This sceptic would end with as many opinions as before, and just as unreliable. But 'treat as false' may also mean 'treat as you would treat a falsehood', i.e. put aside or disregard. "In the search for metaphysically certain truths no more attention should be paid to doubtful items than to those obviously false - and no-one in his right mind could have read it otherwise!"(Replies 7).

The saint who loses his faith need not become an atheist. The rejection of all previous beliefs requires unbelief, not disbelief in the sense of believing something different. The ex-believer need not take on a fresh set of contrary beliefs.

3. INTENTIONAL BELIEF

Any opinion not found completely compelling should, for this once, be deliberately put aside. That is the proposal. But can you decide to believe or disbelieve? If not, then doubting-on-purpose may be a similar absurdity.

One cannot decide to believe in abominable snowmen or in the doctrines of the Creed. Our belief - what we actually think - is constrained by the facts as we find them, and having so found them we cannot decide to find them otherwise. Our vision

5

I.3 Intentional Belief

of the facts may of course be distorted by our prejudice or preference, obscured by ignorance, or made hazy or patchy by carelessness; but none of these factors is deliberate. If Smith consciously <u>tried</u> to think that snowmen do exist, his efforts <u>would</u> ensure that that was not what he really thought (cp Evans, 145f). And if he can't decide what to think, neither can he choose what not to think. Disbelief also cannot be deliberate. So the proposal to go round deliberately disbelieving everything is meaningless.

It is however up to us what we shall say, or do, about what we find we must believe. As theologians put it, we may 'withhold assent' from something that we think is true; either because we are not sure yet, or don't trust our own judgment, or because acting on it looks like being inconvenient. And this applies outside theology as well. No-one can deliberately believe or disbelieve that three lines in a plane must form a triangle, but one can suspend belief while considering if our grounds for it are good enough: that is, one may decide not to act on it for the present, not to rely on other things which flow from it, etc. One can deliberately question a belief.

Why not then say one is questioning beliefs, putting them aside for audit at a stocktaking. Why all this parade of denial, these invented reasons for pretended non-belief? (<u>Objections</u> 5). Because the old familiar opinions will come running back, one relies on them still without even realizing. Freeing oneself of all the errors imbibed since babyhood is not an easy job. Some strong medicine will be needed: just saying that you could be wrong is not enough (<u>Replies</u> 5).

The form of the experiment is clear: trial non-belief in each item of previous belief. Failure marks an item as undisbelievable. The discovery of these items marks the success of the experiment.

I.3 Intentional Belief

The purpose of the experiment was also clear to Descartes:

> I was engaged meanwhile in uprooting from my mind all the mistakes which found their way up till then -- not in imitation of the sceptics who just doubt for doubting's sake, and make out they cannot make up their minds. No, my aim was just the opposite: to achieve conviction. To reject unstable ground and sand, so as to find rock and clay. And this I think I did achieve (<u>Discourse</u> 3).

4. UNREAL DOUBT

C.S.Peirce compared Descartes' doubts to paper currency, which he clearly considered a fiddle and a sham. Enquiry, he held, must always begin from where we are, from our actual set of opinions, our existing beliefs. When one of these comes into conflict with our present reading of experience we are thrown into an uncomfortable hesitancy, a state of real Doubt, resolved only by some revision which reconciles the new experience with what still seems certain of the old; and this revised version then constitutes our new Belief. Doubt, on this view, is something that happens to us, when real opinions genuinely conflict. It is not an experimental suspension of belief.

> This initial doubt will be a mere self-deception ... a person may ... find reason to doubt what he began by believing: but in that case he doubts because he has a positive reason for it, and not on account of the Cartesian maxim. Let us not pretend to doubt in philosophy what we do not doubt in our hearts (Peirce V #265).

Real belief is a habit of mind, a settled tendency to a certain practical response, and cannot be shaken by pretended counter-evidence. That is why professed sceptics still walk up steps and sit on chairs, without precaution or uncertainty. Real doubt would make them hesitate, at least. "So you call it doubting to write down on a piece of paper that you doubt?" (Peirce V #416).

I.4 Unreal Doubt

Descartes went on writing long after denying that there was paper, pen or ink. He does not really think they have vanished, he is only playing 'just suppose'. Peirce derides such theoretical, artificial doubts as meaningless. Yet for some purposes they are unavoidable.

In the procedure called 'indirect proof' the item up for proof is first denied, and that denial is then shown to be unsustainable. For example:

> There is no greatest number. For suppose there were, and call it N. Add 1. The resulting sum, N+1, must be greater than N, the number we just supposed as greater than them all. But that's ridiculous!   Q E D.

Here the Q E D is stated first: 'there is no greatest number'. It is then shown that denying this (by supposing N) would involve asserting N's contrary as well; but that is a contradiction, so it must be wrong. Any item 'reduced to absurdity' like this will just have to be denied, so its contrary (the Q E D) simply must be true, being undeniable-without-absurdity.

Now this indirect proof proceeds by denying something experimentally (the Q E D). The denial does indeed turn out to be contradictory, and so not-properly-assertable; but we shall never find that out if we are not allowed to try. Once concede Peirce's prohibition of artificial doubt, and the whole procedure of <u>reductio</u> becomes impossible.

Some such experimental questioning - let's see what happens if we try denying so-and-so - is involved whenever a conclusion is established by an inference:

> Socrates is wondering if he is mortal. Direct verification seems a little premature. But if he accepts that 'all men are mortal' then surely this general truth will also apply to Socrates?

Logic-books commonly present such reasonings like an addition-sum: premisses first, put two and two together, then see where you are. In practice, we usually think of the conclusion first but with a question-mark:

8

I.4 Unreal Doubt

Socrates, mortal   YES/NO ?

and then look around for facts and principles to prove it or confute it with. If 'Socrates is a man' and 'all men are mortal' are given, then 'Socrates is mortal' will (we are forced to concede) be undeniable. So the conclusion is established by trying to deny it (while affirming the premisses) and finding that we cannot do so with consistency (cp Ree 71).

If such formal and experimental doubt is involved in all deductive inference, then Peirce cannot be right in declaring that doubt is always immediate, practical and personal. And even he makes room for hypothesis:

> Doubt is not usually hesitancy about what is to be done then and there ... every answer to a question that has any meaning is a decision as to how we would act under imagined circumstances (V #375).

Thus if I check in to a picturesque hotel with wooden stairs and narrow winding passages, and then wonder how I might get down in case of fire, my hypothetic dither between Door and Window, if resolved, could well shape my action in a real emergency. Experimental doubt can have immediate and practical effect.

Even playful wondering-if is allowed for:

> I have, for example to wait in a railway-station, and to pass the time I read the advertisements on the walls. I compare the advantages of different trains and different routes which I never expect to take, merely fancying myself to be in a state of hesitancy, because I am bored with having nothing to trouble me. Feigned hesitancy ... plays a great part in the production of scientific enquiry ... when all is over ... we find ourselves decided as to how we should act under such circumstances as those which occasioned our hesitation. In other words, we have attained belief (Peirce V #394, cp Palmer 1981a).

Any doubt is all right, then, so long as it ends up one day in practical belief. And this end

I.4 Unreal Doubt

may be reached by way of trying to doubt something basic and indubitable:

> The original beliefs only remain indubitable in their application to affairs that resemble those of a primitive mode of life ... (but) as soon as we find a belief shows symptoms of becoming instinctive, although it may seem dubitable, we must suspect that experiment would show that it is not really so; for in our artificial life, especially in that of a student, no mistake is more likely than that of taking a paper-doubt for the genuine metal (V #445).

You may think it open to question whether, say, incest is always and absolutely wrong. Alright, try seriously doubting it; and your own reaction may show that belief 'original' and indubitable.

Peirce's trenchant original critique of Cartesian doubt has now disappeared. Like Descartes, he is now practising formal, experimental doubt to discover which doubts are basic and undoubtable. But he favours different tests for being-impossible-to-doubt. For Descartes, this privileged position is assigned only if some sort of contradiction would result from a contrary belief. Pierce takes gut-reaction as sufficient sign that a belief is really 'part of us'.

Descartes' doubts are formal, i.e. without special occasion in his life. Their resolution also is non-personal. They serve to select those beliefs that are logically impossible-to-doubt. This is a purely theoretical thought-experiment. But is there any point in it? Will the result mean anything, make any difference to anyone? That is what Peirce really questioned. This doubt was raised again by Wittgenstein.

5. KNOWING FIRST

Every doubt is based on some previous knowledge or belief, by which to do the questioning.

First of all, the doubter must understand his own expression of his doubt. If George says 'I doubt whether fairies really exist', he must first know what these six words mean, and many more, and

I.5 Knowing First

how they are put together to make a statement or express a doubt:-

> If I wanted to doubt that this is my hand, then how could I help doubting whether the word 'hand' means anything? I know that, apparently (Wittgenstein #369, cf #306).

The same point is acknowledged by Descartes:

> When I stated that this proposition 'I think, therefore I am' is the first and most certain ... I did not deny that we must first of all know what is knowledge, what is existence and what is certainty (<u>Principles</u> I.x).

Of course we may mistake the meaning of a word: many would mis-define 'serendipity', and their statements would probably be inappropriate in consequence. But if such error or uncertainty spread to many common words then communication would simply break down. (For a practical test of this, try curling the right edge of the paper as you read, and see how many words per line you can lose and still catch the sense.)

Words and meanings apart, many facts must be accepted before we can begin to doubt: just as you need to come across many sets of similar things, before you can make a start on counting them. Counting and doubting are complex, reflective operations, undertaken in a context of familiarity. One might well advise a boy "Yes, you <u>can</u> stand up in a boat, but don't do it on Day One!". Thus a pupil who interrupts constantly to ask if the Past is Real, or whether there is any Nature for the scientists to investigate, is told "Your doubts don't yet make any sense"; i.e. learn the stuff first, then you can begin to question it; you need some expertise to know which doubts are relevant (Wittgenstein #310, cp #160).

In some areas of life the business of challenging has a quite specific range and function, and is conducted by explicit rules. Some games have their own peculiar challenges: thus L B W is at home in cricket, but nowhere else. Perhaps the same applies to "Is it really so?", a challenge found in certain language-games, which may not work outside those games, or make sense when applied to everything-in-general (cp Wittgenstein #3, #24).

I.5 Knowing First

By contrast, consider the notion of fair play. Some common sorts of fair and foul play will be mentioned in any set of rules, but never all of them: the wit of man can always devise some dirty trick which has not yet formally been prohibited. And people will always debate whether it is fair play or not. For example, if the losing side all sit down on the ball until the final whistle goes, to secure a draw, shall we say this cannot be foul play because it has never been prohibited? Only a very dedicated legalist would find that satisfactory. Here the critical notion of fair play is seen at work not only to disqualify misdeeds specified in the rules which constitute that particular game, but also applying to cases not covered by those rules. It could even be used quite 'in general', for assessing a given set of rules.

It may still be said that doubt is at home in certain specific language-games: not in all, and not between them, or 'in general'. To some, this statement seems self-evident. Others will seek to support it, either as a peculiar fact about doubt or as following from the nature of a language-game.

As to games properly so called, all recognize some degree of overlap. Bat and ball are for cricket, knights and pawns for chess, shuttles for badminton ... ; nets and racquets, however, are less particular, scoring is widespread, winning, losing and doing it for fun are completely general. It is difficult to argue that because doubt comes into games A and B and C it can have no place in other intellectual activities.

'Language-game' is a made-up term of art, suggesting an analogy which is striking in places and fairly weak at other points. One suggestion is to carve linguistic activities up into distinct segments which are then declared 'autonomous'. And few will deny that heckling, praying in public and bidding for sticks of furniture are distinct activities, each with its own conventions and terminology. But any negative argument of the sort "X belongs to A and therefore not to B" requires definite and reliable boundaries, which language and convention do not always indicate. A society relying on such argument will then require a cadre of line-drawers outside and above the activities delimited: an overall, 'general' occupation, often called philosophy, and of just the character the game-analogy was originally intended to exclude (cp Palmer 1968, and <u>Analogy</u> 115f).

If the lines cannot be definitely drawn then the game of re-stating things in terms of language-games is just another version of the pragmatist test: What is the living point and use of general doubt? Will it make any real difference to anything? The aim of Descartes' universal doubting-game is to pick out those beliefs for which supremely good reasons can be found. Some people find this game worth playing. They notice a difference between the examined and the unexamined life. From that finding, made by those who have themselves tried both, there should be no appeal, at least for pragmatists like Wittgenstein.

Only one thing counts as making sure, in this doubting-game: seeing one couldn't possibly think different. Descartes did not invent this very strict criterion, but took it over from the great mediaeval reasoners, whose proofs were mainly indirect. Thus if someone asks what reasons we have to suppose that two and two make four, we answer by showing that any other sum would have consequences which conflict <u>with each other</u>. Descartes went further, and considered answers whose consequences conflict <u>with our giving them</u>; e.g. one answer to the question 'Do I exist?' would have prevented my ever asking it. Descartes was thus relaxing the metaphysical criterion, and admitting a wider range of arguably certain truths.

6. INVESTIGATIVE DOUBT

The doubt which Descartes proposed was to apply to each belief in turn but not to all of them at once. It was to apply temporarily, for purposes of experiment. The experiment was to pick out those items which could not be doubted, i.e. those which we got into contradiction by trying to deny. If this selection of privileged 'necessary beliefs' is worth having, and can be discovered in this way, then the experiment is worth doing. A 'general' doubt pursued in this way for these purposes makes perfectly good sense.

A philosopher anxious for an audience will sometimes suggest that his philosophic doubts could

I.6 Investigative Doubt

undermine all our ordinary purposes. And no doubt it is true that IF there were no natures or laws of connection, no solid continuing things, no sense in events or soundness in memory or truth conveyed by inference, IF I could be the only person anywhere and all others in my dream and maybe me as well THEN cricket and gardening, physics, accountancy, even sitting-down would be at risk. The name 'sceptical' is usually given to these preposterous hypotheses.

Sceptics are like dragons. You never actually meet one, but keep on running across heroes who have just fought with them, and won. As a thought-out position, a genuine World-view, such scepticism is empty of content and without protagonists. But it makes a handy Aunt Sally to aim our refutations at, and provides a suitably synthetic distress for the knights of knowledge to rescue damsels from (cp Bieri 1977).

The serious questions confusingly dramatized in such talk are these: Which of our beliefs are basic and unchangeable? What good reasons have we to rely on them? One way towards an answer is to consider dispensing with some or all of them. This thought-experiment should sort them out, and put a price-tag on each one - the cost of not having this or that belief.

Both Peirce and Wittgenstein thought some beliefs basic and unchangeable, as a matter of fact, for each one of us. Wittgenstein thought there were a lot of them; for him, doubting is a specialized operation at the edges of the fabric of belief. Peirce, like Collingwood, thought we could tell which of Smith's beliefs were undoubtable-for-Smith by noting Smith's reaction to our attempt to question them (Peirce V #445; Collingwood 31). For both writers, there is a basic belief-set for each person and (more or less) for each culture or each age. We can't get outside our local, current one, to see if that set is well-grounded, true or justified, for these are questions that we cannot even ask.

Descartes also thought some beliefs would turn out basic; basic for everyone, in every age and clime, because they simply had to be true. Which ones were really basic could be made out by trying to reject them, and getting bruised in the attempt. This programme is, no doubt, initially presented as

I.6 Investigative Doubt

a spring-clean of the lumber room; but he never pays much attention to what he throws away. His interest is not in the detectable falsities of life - that toadstools are left about by fairies, that sugar dissolved does really disappear. Rather, he is engaged in distinguishing two sorts of truth. Some true beliefs can be treated-as-false: to treat them so is incorrect, of course, but it is possible. Others cannot. Those which cannot are well worth picking out. They are not all obvious at sight. Doubt is the reagent which reveals their character, for these indubitables actually give off a contradiction when experimentally denied.

Scepticism of this investigative sort seems eminently sensible.

Chapter Two

THE COGITO

Descartes proposed doubting each of his beliefs in turn, to pick out some of them as undeniable. This did not involve him in professing the opposite of each, nor in deliberately choosing what he would believe, but in trying to suspend judgment; an experiment worth trying if only to see just when it would not work.

The next move in that game is to argue some things undeniable because established by our failure in denying them. This indirect, 'transcendental' line of argument is now to be analyzed, in the first famous paradigm case, the <u>Cogito</u>.

7. <u>A</u>, SO <u>B</u>

It was all a big mistake, just everything; or so I tried to think. But that meant my being something, to be thinking it. My thinking means my being there: this truth, so definitive and so reliable, could be taken ... as basic for my new philosophy (<u>Discourse</u> 4).

Somewhere or other, for each one of us, the doubting has to stop. For Descartes, it stopped at his being there to think: the only point he could positively prove, without assuming anything.

The proof seems simple, and everyone is sure he follows it. It is when they explain how it works that the disagreement starts. Some even query if it was put forward as a proof: might not "I exist" be just a simple fundamental truth, a principle so basic and obvious that all higher, further truths could be safely built on it?

II.7 A, so B

A proof is certainly different from a principle. They serve different purposes, and need to pass quite different tests. Yet in wording they can be very similar. Each argument must have its own principle, to work from; but we may not bother to state that principle every time we use the argument. Thus - to take quite a different example - suppose young Johnny is dashing out, and his mother calls "It's raining, you'll get wet". Two separate, factual statements; A, B. B has not happened yet. It may never happen: that depends on what young Johnny does, which in turn may be influenced, his mother hopes, by his connecting A with B. "It's raining <u>so</u> you will get wet" is what she was really meaning to convey.

Johnny can see that it's raining. The 'so' can only be gathered from the experience of going in the rain and getting wet. The connection of thought thus rests upon a factual principle. With that spelt out in full, her message would have run:

You get wet if you go out in the rain.
It is raining.
So if you go out now you will get wet.

But if she means all this, then why not say it all? Because Johnny would be out of earshot, before she reached the point. She must cut her message down to bare essentials, like a telegram; he knows he hasn't a coat on, he knows what happens, going out without - he's not quite an idiot - and he knows he's going out. And never mind the 'so', just let him work that out, it might slow him down a bit. So she actually says "It's raining. You'll get wet".

Does all this analysis help? Why bother inventing extra words she may have thought but did not say? It won't help Johnny, once he's got the point. But it may help us to see how that point is reached, by a particular puzzling bit of reasoning.

But isn't it risky, all this make-up first, smoothing out unwelcome wrinkles and pencilling in lines to say what we desire? Might we not easily go wrong, and put a false face on the argument? Yes, it is risky. But then, not doing it is risky too. If there are logical insights to be lost by a mistaken analysis, we shall certainly lose them by not attempting it at all.

II.7 A, so B

The insight offered by our invented extra words is this: the mother is moving from 'rain' to 'getting wet', by an unstated factual principle which connects the two: "if it rains you'll get wet going out". This principle sounds very like the inference "as it's raining you'll get wet going out"; and this similarity in wording helps to explain why rapid reasoners often leave out one of them. But checking the facts stated in a principle is quite different from checking the application of that principle in an inference. So we had better state them separately when it comes to assessment and anlysis.

In the case of the <u>Cogito</u>, principle and inference look very similar, but we can distinguish them by putting in quotation marks:

(principle) "I think" implies that I exist.
(inference) I think. Therefore, I exist.

We cannot tell whether Descartes would have put them in, as this handy symbol was not then in common use.

Descartes expected the <u>Cogito</u> to provide "the first principle of my new philosophy," yet he recognized that a mere connection was not enough to build a system on:

> When I said that "I think so I am" is the first and most certain ... I did not deny that we must first know what knowledge is and existence ... and that in order to think we must exist: but as these are the very simplest of notions and tell us nothing about what exists, I did not put them down (<u>Principles</u> I.x).

The connection 'thinking involves existing' is not sufficient by itself, though it will serve as the 'principle' or major premiss of an argument: an argument that would have no force at all, without that connecting principle.

To start a system, Descartes requires proof: a principle, and a fact, and then an inference. Let us look for these.

8. THOUGHTS NEED THINKERS

Descartes means to establish beyond doubt that he, Descartes, does exist. That is the point to be proved, the Q E D of the Cogito. The argument starts from the fact that Descartes is thinking this or that. Of course he might be wrong in what he thinks; he might think of that river there as the Isis when it is the Cherwell after all. But even making a mistake requires thought. However wrong he may be, it remains right that he is thinking so and so.

In arguing from this thought to his being there he appeals to a principle: that in order to think, we must already exist (Principle I.x). He finds this out for himself: that unless he personally existed he personally could not be thinking anything (Replies 2). "You could gather as much" said Gassendi, "from anything you do. Anything which does, must be. That is self-evident" (Objections 5). Descartes replied that other actions would not do. For only thought is absolutely, metaphysically certain. I could not prove my body by arguing from "I walk", though "I think I walk" would show reliably that a mind was there (Replies 5).

This reply makes clear that Descartes is using argument, and seeking proof. And proof does not result if the premisses are dubious. You could be wrong in thinking that you walk, but clearly just by thinking it, you think. This grants that 'I exist' does follow just as well from other verbs. So we have a large class of parallel principles: thinking means existing, walking means existing, shaving means existing ... in general, doing anything means being there, to be doing it.

These principles are true and obvious to everyone. But what makes them true, and why are they so obvious? To make this out, we shall need to begin with a fairly general case, and then see what extra features come in as we make it more particular. Take a short police-court drama:

George hit Bill

Clearly some George is essential to the action, in this case. So if it is true that George hit Bill then there must be some George about, and indeed

19

II.8 Thoughts need Thinkers

some Bill. If the charge is more specific:

George broke Bill's glasses with a coconut

Bill will require spectacles and George will need a coconut. Now the question arises, if coconuts were not available, might not George have done it with a turnip just as well? If so, the instrument will appear less vital to the action than does the agent, George. Alternatively, we may hold that 'hitting with a coconut' is a different action from using a turnip. But we cannot regard these both as simply different from 'George hit Bill'. Rather, they are more specific, it more general. There are more actions still to be gathered under the formula 'George hit ...' and still more under '... hit ... ' or under merely 'George ... ... '(One attraction of <u>John Brown's Body</u> ... is the licence it grants us to imagine things).

   To a particular action, then, all its constituents must be held essential, equally. But we do tend to organize them in a certain way: hittings, George's hittings, George's hittings of Bill ... This order of convenience: verb, subject, object, then etceteras, suggests that the agent is vital to the action while the rest are variable and dispensable. This suggestion is reinforced by the actions called intransitive, such as 'George smokes'. In fact, he must smoke something: a pipe, a cigar, a cigarette ... But in society, and railway-carriages, only his output matters, so we leave the generic statement and treat it as complete. Of course chimneys also smoke, so one cannot infer from ' ... smokes' to an individual agent such as George. But if the whole action is given, as in 'George smokes', then it will have to be true that there is some George.

   May we then argue from action to agent, from the fact that George smokes to some needful George? We do so argue, when his actions are given to us on authority. For example, a neighbour may tell us of some nearby gardening: how George dug this and watered that, sprayed all around and even tidied up: and if we believe her stories we shall certainly infer some George for them to be about. But if we doubt her word, and keep watch from the back window to verify her statements one by one, we shall always find we have established his existence on the way. Thus the existential inference to 'there must be a

20

II.8 Thoughts need Thinkers

George' is superfluous whenever the premiss 'George did it' is available. The inference from action to agent is valid, no doubt: but you can't need it when it's usable. And people don't use it except where the action is given on authority, at second-hand, as in scriptures and histories and neighbours' narratives.

Suppose now someone accuses George, saying "You hit Bill". Here the action requires an agent, as before; and in this case a sufferer as well, called Bill. And the accusation needs a defendant, namely George; and an accuser too (unspecified), for accusing is another action, and requires an agent and a patient or sufferer. So from an accusation, if made, we can reliably infer some accuser and an accusee. And people do so infer, on reading in the newspaper that "a serious accusation of negligence was made in the County Court today". For accusations don't just happen on their own, not even in newspapers or on Court premisses. There has to be someone in there doing it.

Here again the inference is based on testimony: the newspaper, we suppose, would hardly mention an 'accusation' unless someone were accusing somebody. Unless we can rely on the newspaper to this extent, the inference will fail. And if we had first to make sure for ourselves that an accusation really did take place, we should in the process discover who was accusing whom: and the inference to these parties would become superfluous.

Suppose now George confesses, "I hit Bill". The action George is confessing to needs an agent and a sufferer. The confession also requires confessor and recipient. But the agent is the confessor. George's presence is required twice. If we hear the confession, for example spoken behind us on the bus, we shall certainly infer some George or other to have done the hitting and be speaking of it afterwards. But our inference will still depend on hearsay. It could be that what we overheard was false, or was said in jest, or had reference to a game of billiards. Not but what we could turn around and question our vocal George: Was Bill himself actually hit? Was George's confession to be taken literally? Was he serious? But by the time we have verified these points our inference, now totally reliable, will be totally superfluous.

II.8 Thoughts need Thinkers

An unhappy alternative thus confronts anyone inferring from action to agent: either the premisses are hearsay and unreliable, or they are verified already and so have rendered the inference superfluous. In particular, the action of saying or thinking so-and-so does imply some speaker or thinker as agent, but that agent if dubious cannot be established by such an inference. For no-one can verify "I think", not even I, without thereby making sure that I exist.

9. SOLILOQUOY

'I exist' is derivable from 'I think', but only by a specious argument: the inference is valid, but could not make the conclusion more believable. For 'I think' is not and cannot be available for proving 'I exist', since that conclusion would be needed first, in arriving at the premisses. One may hold up one end of a plank, or else climb up on it if supported otherwise: but one cannot hold it up while climbing on.

As far as the inference goes, one could just as well start from 'I walk' or 'I feel like a sneeze'. Descartes granted such inference, but thought his starting-point was more reliable, as 'I think' seems certain even in those extreme cases where 'I walk' is not. Now, why does it seem certainer?

The third-person statement 'George hit Bill' could fail for lack of referee (no George) or of object (no Bill). In the vaguer 'George got violent' no object is specified, thus eliminating failure for lack of object, at the price of saying rather less. Both statements need stat-ers (makers), if really truly made, and both seem to need an audience.

In first-person soliloquoy, the statement-maker also serves as audience, and then doubles up as referee: once the statement is made, maker and audience and referee are guaranteed. This does not show the statement true: one may have George and Bill to hand and it still be false that George hit Bill. Their availability only excludes failure for lack of reference.

II.9 Soliloquoy

Self-reference may seem a guarantee of truth. But consider a town map, put up in a public place to help the visitors, and bearing an arrow with the legend YOU ARE HERE. Where is 'here'? Where the arrow points to, which is (or should be) where the map has been set up. Who is 'you'? The visitor who is looking at the map. So he is where the map is: that much is guaranteed. And the map should be located at the place indicated by the arrow on the map. But if the arrow has been marked in wrong, then where the map is will not be where the arrow on the map is pointing to. Or maybe the draughtsman got the arrow right but then the council workmen went and installed the map in some other place, so that the place where the map actually is (with our benighted visitor consulting it) is not the place which the point on the map that the arrow actually points to does actually represent. So the best we can say to reassure our worried visitor is that IF the map is in the right place AND IF the arrow is in the right place on the map THEN the place it points to is the place occupied by the visitor who looks at it. As visitors are easily reassured this reassurance may suffice; but with so many IFs his position is hardly guaranteed (cp Boyle 1972).

Soliloquizers have their guarantee of reference, but can still say something wrong about themselves. Is there then some further feature in 'I think', to make it seem so reliable?

If George, coming home, calls out "Where are you, Jane?" she may answer "I'm here", which has to be true but does not exactly answer him. Of course he may learn what he wanted, if he can recognize the voice and tell where it is coming from: though it could still be a ghost or a parrot, a tape-recording or a much-practised member of the kidnap gang. But it's true! Yes, whoever says it (if it is indeed said), and wherever that speaker is, that's where that speaker is, and that's all that speaker has actually said about anything. So the answer, while it may convey information just by being made, does not in itself have any to convey. Its truth is an empty trick, based upon a supposed self-reference.

In the same way 'I think' is guaranteed true by the fact of my considering its truth or falsity: whatever I may be thinking and whoever I may be, thinking is what I must be doing when thinking that I think. But it seems an empty achievement. We

23

II.9 Soliloquoy

would hardly commend a Wodehouse baronet for truthfulness if he never got beyond "I say ..., I say ...".

Even the briefest self-referring soliloquoy will usually do more than merely self-refer. The 'speaker' will indicate to himself some action or thought of a certain well-known individual, age so-and-so, hair colour such-and-such, born at a certain town and having certain facial peculiarities he could recognize in the mirror any time ... Knowing this individual quite well, he does not use the name but the pronoun 'I'. For him, in that context, that pronoun carries all the individualizing background information normally conveyed and presumed in a proper name.

We may of course reject this personalized packaging of utterance, strip off the time and the place and all the identifying individuality, and attend solely to what is said, "I ...". Would we still understand, or only think we did, by analogy with other pronominal references whose referees are real worldly individuals? If we strip the onion too much the 'I' that seemed to be inside may disappear.

The "I think" of Descartes is formally guaranteed by providing an instance of itself whenever he really thinks of it; just as "I say" and "Here" are guaranteed true when personally said (though not when reproduced mechanically or imitated by a talking bird). The 'I' can just refer to whoever is doing it, in an empty and reliable self-reference; or it may mean a distinct nameable individual who goes on long enough to have a conversation with himself, in which case the statement is informative and dubious. That R. Descartes engaged in mental activity on, say, October 4th 1636 at 10 p.m. is a factual matter, which cannot be formally guaranteed.

Soliloquoy does eliminate some ways of going wrong: not all. Self-reference in soliloquoy is formally guaranteed, but is then empty, the 'I' just marking a place for the speaker, but not referring to any actual individual. For a full and natural self-reference appeal must be made to information outside the given utterance, e.g. to memories.

It is, moreover, an odd procedure to start out from soliloquoy. The activity of specific,

II.9 Soliloquoy

articulated 'thought' may well have developed out of 'speaking to oneself', and so may presuppose the public activity of speaking-to-others both as an earlier, more basic skill and as a conceptual prerequisite (cp #41b, below). However that may be, any Charles who offers to tell us, publicly, about some private George whose speech might be always only to himself will owe us an account of how he, Charles, could be telling us this, on George's supposed scheme of things. We can put up with one solipsist at a time, not two. So while the premiss 'I think' does seem more certain, in soliloquoy, that is more than compensated by our increased difficulty of access, as ultimate audience to the soliloquoy.

The inference from "I think" to "I exist" is an inference from action to agent. The premiss seems certain because 'I' is self-reflexive, like 'here', and equally uninformative; and because 'think' is taken as completely general; so that even in being deceived you 'think'.

The premiss (plus the principle that actions need agents) does validly imply that this vague empty 'I' does in a minimal mental spoofy way 'exist'. But this implication is not available for use in a proof, because the conclusion is needed when establishing the premisses.

10. REFLECTIVE CERTAINTY

Now it may be urged that mental acts are only known, and are fully known 'from the inside'. Only George can finally tell if George is inferring, supposing, wondering ...; and if George thinks he is, he is. Enjoying this confidence, George will hardly need Descartes' argument to reassure himself that he exists (cp Chisholm 1979).

On this traditional theory, you first notice that you are digging or dithering, then recognize 'yourself' as doer of these deeds. Self-knowledge is reflective: you don't see yourself directly, but only in the mirror of your deeds. In another way it is immediate, something 'just-seen' (intuited) all at once, without intervening reasoning. Descartes accepted this theory at first: "each individual can mentally have intuition of the fact that he exists and that he thinks" (<u>Rules</u> 3).

II.10 Reflective Certainty

The <u>Cogito</u> seems to spell out this intuition in an inference: deeds need doers, here is one certain deed for which a doer is required. To this we object that if the conclusion needs support it cannot acquire it by this line of reasoning, for then the premisses would be needing it as well. Either that particular premiss is unreliable, or else the inference must be superfluous.

Does this adverse assessment of the <u>Cogito</u> make much real difference? It does to Descartes, for he built a lot on it. Dramatically, he needs the <u>Cogito</u> to turn the tide of universal doubt. In real terms, he needs it as proof, to provide a nucleus of a privileged class of 'provables'. And he hopes to show that "it's really a thinker that I am" (<u>sum res cogitans</u>). These projects will all collapse if the <u>Cogito</u> is not reliable as proof.

We may still, of course, enjoy a reflective acquaintance with our inner states and with ourselves: my nose is itching, my leg aches, my conscience troubles me, I love figure-skating and solving crosswords, tobogganing <u>is</u> fun - and there's me liking and doing and hating all those things. This reflective certainty remains, and does feel certain, at least until you reflect on it. Only the proposed proof has been shown unreliable (cp Zemach 1975, Pompa 1984).

  *   *   *   *

Interpreting the great dead is always a perilous affair. When all the texts have been cited the background investigated and the influences traced the interpreter can only say "I <u>think</u> our author meant to reason thus and so - and I offer these comments on that reasoning".

We have tried to evaluate one version of the <u>Cogito</u>. We are unlikely now to discover whether Descartes also thought of it. Never mind: for it can help us on our way to understanding transcendental argument.

Chapter Three

WHAT THE COGITO REFUTES

Descartes was doubting everything, to see if any belief was quite impregnable. The Cogito seemed such a one, and others might later be welcomed back by the same criterion. In stating this line of thought he did not always trouble to distinguish the inference itself from the principle which governed it: that thoughts need thinkers. The other premiss, 'I think', seems guaranteed by being so general and being said about oneself; but it cannot be relied on until the conclusion is reliable, which (if we are relying on that inference) means relying on those premisses. The argument goes round and back again to its starting-point, and can never prove "I think".

We must now try to trace out the steps in this roundabout line of reasoning. For while it cannot prove its conclusion it may, in a way, refute the contrary: and it was to refute a sceptical doubt that the argument was introduced.

11. p-CIRCULARITY

It is often said that Descartes "begs the question" in the Cogito, a rather unsporting thing to do, not closely specified but somehow linked with circularity. Let us try to describe more precisely the defect we have already detected in his argument, and then see what is left of his programme for philosophy.

An argument is circular if its conclusion figures among its premisses: C, A, B ⟶ C. When Descartes inferred a God from his own clear idea of one, his critics remarked that he would need a God,

III.11 p-Circularity

first, to guarantee his clear ideas as reliable; i.e. they complained of circularity (<u>Meditation</u> 3, cp <u>Objections</u> 2 and reply, <u>Replies</u> 4).

Any circular argument is valid: if the premisses are true then so is the conclusion, for it is one of them, and surely the conclusion follows from itself! The other premisses serve only as a smokescreen, to conceal this from the arguers.

If the premisses of a circular argument are all reliable, then so will its conclusion be. Conversely, if the conclusion is uncertain, then so are the premisses, collectively. So a conclusion which needs establishing cannot be established by premisses including it, as that premiss-set still needs establishing. A pillar can support a roof, from underneath, while standing on the ground: but not, by standing on the roof.

Now consider an incomplete argument, for example "Everything the Bible says is true, see 2 Timothy 3.16". We look it up and read "all scripture is inspired by God". Does that mean all of it is true? Well, suppose we grant that anything God says is true. That brings us to "the writer to Timothy says that what any scripture says is true". But why should we take his word for it? Perhaps his bishop will write him a reference, saying that he is very sound, doctrinally. Or we might ourselves decide to rely on everything he says, acting on information received direct from the Archangel Gabriel. Failing these extraordinary assurances, we shall probably fall back on the fact that this letter itself is contained in the Bible, and "everything the Bible says is true".

The argument is now complete - and circular, for the conclusion has been used to bolster up the premisses. And the connection is a valid one: IF the conclusion were reliable THEN the premiss which equals it would also be; and IF the premiss-set were genuinely guaranteed THEN so would the conclusion have to be. But this see-saw of would-be reliability cannot <u>make</u> the conclusion reliable.

There are of course many incomplete arguments which can be completed without turning into roundabouts, since independent evidence is available for establishing their premisses. We are concerned with the others: with those few remarkable arguments

III.11 p-Circularity

where such evidence is not available, so that their premisses can be collectively established only by their conclusion's aid. Such arguments may be called 'presumptively circular', or p-circular for short.

The argument "George smokes, so he exists" is p-circular, as one could not establish the fact that George smokes without using the fact that he exists. The inference runs back over ground already won - if it has been really won.

The argument "I think, so I exist" also moves backwards, from 'me thinking' to one of its elements, the 'me'. If this 'me' is really at question no answer can be supplied by such an argument, unless we could somehow be given 'me thinking' independently of 'me'. But if we are given 'me thinking' then we have been given 'me' and do not need to establish it by any sort of argument.

Mummy, look at my picture.
Very good. What's it meant to be?
It's me painting. There's the paper and the paints and the paint-brushes ...
And where are you?
Oh, I've just gone away for a moment.

How can the picture show him painting if he isn't in it, but has 'gone away'? And how could you display 'me thinking' independently of 'me'?

Circularity in argument can be formally defined, by the unusual arrangement of having the conclusion included among the premisses. This relation ensures that the argument is valid, for the conclusion can hardly be false if all the premisses are true. It also ensures that the argument is 'epistemically' unsound, i.e. no good for knowing anything; for if all the premisses are known already then so is the conclusion (being one of them), and argument becomes superfluous, while if at the outset the conclusion is uncertain then the premisses are not all known so inference cannot begin.

We call an argument p-circular if

(i) it is incomplete, and
(ii) it cannot be completed without importing circularity.

29

III.11 p-Circularity

Circularity and incompleteness are readily definable and easy to detect, whereas 'cannot be completed without ...' is negative, and more debatable. In practice, a challenge will suffice: "Please show me this premiss established <u>independently</u> of the conclusion, or else give up appealing to that argument".

This challenge is 'epistemic' in character. It concerns the order in which we get to know the premiss in question, A, and the conclusion, C. If you can't make sure that A is true without on the way making sure that C is too, then there's no use in deploying A as part of an argument for guaranteeing C. So the challenge is, to show A true <u>without</u> appeal to C. It is not a question of <u>whether</u> A can be true without C being true as well. That question relates to the underlying facts, not to our ways and means of knowing them. In any valid argument the premisses can't be true unless the conclusion is so too: but our question is, can the premiss be <u>known</u> first? (cp Note A to #14 below)

So far, we have considered positive, direct proof of a conclusion, C. But the same conclusion might also be confirmed indirectly, by showing its contrary, not-C, to be untenable. Can p-circular arguments serve in refutations of this sort?

12. REFUTATION

Given three propositions A, B, C, combined into a simple argument (A, B so C), we can form a 'triad' which asserts the first two and denies the third (A,B,not-C). The truth of this triad would serve as a counter-instance to the argument, for if A, B, and not-C can all be true together then the truth of C could not follow from that of A and B. And if the argument <u>is</u> valid then A, B, not-C cannot all be jointly true: if two are true the other must be false. This 'inconsistency' can serve, in reverse, to show the validity of the argument: if A, B, not-C <u>cannot</u> be jointly true then A,B so C must be a valid argument. Now inconsistency can sometimes be perceived without considering the actual truth or falsity of the constituent elements, A, B, C. In this way we might come to see that one of them must be wrong, without yet knowing which.

III.12 Refutation

This relation can be used in proof, three ways: Given that (A, B, not-C) is inconsistent, we may argue

(1) A, B are true so not-C is false

(2) B, not-C are true so A is false

(3) not-C, A are true so B is false

Such proofs require premisses known first and independently, and are disabled by circularity. Thus if B can't be known without appeal to C, proof (1) becomes unusable; and so one.

The same relation of inconsistency will also serve to rule out a certain set of views as incompatible. Thus anyone adopting A and B can be required to eschew not-C 'on pain of inconsistency'. Alternatively, he may keep B and elect to say not-C if only he be willing to abandon A. And so on.

This very obvious point becomes significant in a case where actual straightforward inference is inhibited for fear of circularity. Take the triad

A   If I think then I exist
B   I do think
not-C I do not exist

This triad is inconsistent: i.e. the <u>Cogito</u> is a valid argument. So the belief-set (A, B, not-C) is untenable as a whole. But this does not tell us which belief is to be given up; though if we already stand committed to both A and B we can take warning not to combine them with not-C. And this warning does not itself rest on any claim that A and B are known as true, so the complaint of circularity does not arise.

What will this warning do for Smith? On most days, nothing. But if one day he were to try his hand at doubting everything, including C, he could then be warned against denying C while still professing A and B. The creed "I think but I do not exist" is not available for confession, at least not in a world where consistency is prized (cp Boyle 1972).

13. UNDENIABLES

Hobbes remarked that "Knowledge of the proposition 'I exist' does certainly follow or depend on the proposition 'I think' "(<u>Objections</u> 3). On our view, the truth does follow but the knowledge can't. 'I think' could not possibly be right if 'I exist' were wrong, so anyone committed to the first had better concede the second also, for consistency. But knowledge that I exist cannot be obtained from knowledge that I think, being its constituent and so required first. The proof of existence from thought must fail for circularity.

There is however one central passage in which Descartes may be pursuing a different line of thought, not subject to p-circularity:

> Nothing is real, in the whole wide world; no sky, no earth, no minds, no bodies; so I was now convinced. No me? But there must be, for me to be convinced of anything. But what about that deceiver, superbly skilful and all-powerful, all the time fooling me deliberately? If he does fool me then there just has to be a 'me' for him to fool ... so 'I am' just has to be true whenever I say it or think of it (<u>Meditations</u> 2).

According to Hintikka, this passage does not present an inference but a 'performatory' certitude: that 'I exist' just has to be true, if said or thought, since 'I do not exist' would be an inconsistent thing to say (Hintikka 1962).

It may be doubted if this interpretation is true to Descartes as we know him in his texts. As a <u>re</u>-interpretation it has more to offer us. For it shows us something both valuable and sound in his line of reasoning, and so helps to explain why so many have been taken in for so long by so obvious a fallacy.

The historical question may be taken first.

The Latin formula now universally employed, <u>Cogito ergo sum</u>, is found in the <u>Principles</u> of 1644. It is not in the <u>Meditations</u>, though it does appear, in French, in <u>Discourse</u> 4, in a pre-publication abstract of the <u>argument</u> <u>Meditations</u> was later to provide. Of course the author might have changed his mind after the abstract had appeared. But in the <u>Letter to Clerselier</u>, in a summary of his own replies to Gassendi's objections, he writes

> Your friends mark six objections to Meditation Two. The first is that in the statement "I think so I exist" the author of these criticisms will have it ...

This suggests that <u>Cogito ergo sum</u> was to its author a fair summary of the thought presented in Meditations 2. And when Hobbes 'agrees' that knowledge that I exist depends on knowledge that I think (<u>Objections</u> 2) Descartes fails to dissent, though he was always quick to reject a comment as misplaced. This must count against Hintikka's suggestion that in Meditations 2 Descartes is pursuing (dimly, and part-time) a new and quite different line of thought.

Descartes does indeed deny that his <u>Cogito</u> follows a syllogistic form of reasoning. For a syllogism would require as major premiss some general statement such as "everything that thinks exists", which seems too big a helping to be on his plate when he is dieting (<u>Replies</u> 2). And if some previous syllogism were put forward to confirm the point, he would need to remember having seen it proved, when working on the <u>Cogito</u>; which reliance on memory is not permissible until God's goodness has been proved in Meditations 3. To evade these objections Descartes claims that each individual learns that principle by finding in his own case that he could not possibly think and not exist.

Descartes does not deny, in this passage, what he elsewhere grants: that the <u>Cogito</u> is an inference ('this reasoning' <u>Search after Truth</u>, 'infer' <u>Replies</u> 5, in reply to Gassendi, who had only said 'gather'; 'my conclusion' <u>Principles</u> I.ix). He does claim, in the passage cited just above, that

> When we notice that it is thinkers that we are, this is a basic idea not arrived at by syllogistic argument; nor does someone who says "I think so I am" deduce the existence from the thought by a syllogism, but recognises it like something self-evident, by a simple mental look-see (<u>Replies</u> 2).

III.13 Undeniables

But in the 'geometrically presented' arguments appended to these replies, he has a syllogism "whose conclusion can be self-evident to those free from preconceived ideas ... but as such clear vision is not easy to achieve we seek the same result in other ways" (Proposition 1). So one may argue for what is - or ought to be - self-evident!

These tiresome citations show that Descartes did not in these passages say that the Cogito was not an inference, but only that it was not a syllogistic one. His remarks are not always clear, and of course he may have said different things at different times. However, if it is possible so to take his various remarks as to make them consistent with each other and with the facts they refer to, this interpretation is to be preferred.

In any case, Descartes saw no great divide between an 'intuition' and a reasoning. Long arguments with complicated steps were, he thought, to be avoided, if only because they involve relying on the memory. A good reasoner will simplify and organize the steps, and practise leaping several at a time until, perhaps, he can clear the whole lot at a single bound. "This method will both relieve the memory, diminish the sluggishness of our thinking, and definitely enlarge our mental capacity" (Rules 7, cp Discourse 2). An intuition, then, is what such Yoga may turn your inference into if you hold your breath and keep your eye on it and nothing else.

14. STATS

The thoughts Hintikka is introducing to Descartes do have a value of their own. He remarks that certain statements are shown to be false by the fact of their being made: thus if De Gaulle says "De Gaulle does not exist" this 'existentially inconsistent' statement must be false, and so verifies its contradictory. So "De Gaulle exists" must be true (whenever stated by De Gaulle). Hintikka calls such statements 'performatory', i.e. made true just by being made. Now if "I exist" in this way verifies itself, there is no need to infer it from "I think".

Let us call such a self-verifying utterance a 'stat' (like a 'fiat', but indicative). Stats may be simple or complex in structure, easy or difficult

III.14 Stats

to think about. The truth of a difficult complex one may not be obvious at first; the verification although entirely internal may yet require reasoning to work it out, as do difficult riddles with simple answers, like "this man's father was my father's son". So the verification of a stat may not be immediate; it may require inference. Hintikka's neat title "Inference or Performance" thus poses a false alternative.

De Gaulle's supposed stat "I, De Gaulle, exist" can be confirmed by two different reasonings. One is to consider its contradictory, "I, De Gaulle, do not exist" and perceive its peculiar absurdity: this is an indirect proof, a <u>reductio</u>. The other way is to say "I, De Gaulle think I exist, so I do", which was Descartes' reasoning. The position then is this: the <u>Cogito</u> presents one inference, and Hintikka has thought of another leading to the same result.

The term 'existential inconsistency' refers to the subject (De Gaulle) having to exist in order to do so and so. There are also some statements which falsify themselves by being the opposite of what they say; and some non-existential statements which display their own evidence by providing an instance of that which they allege:

    Mother No need to shout, dear
    Johnny I'm NOT SHOUTING (a bellow)
    Mother (barely audible) Well, I'm whispering

The making of these remarks provides instances to falsify or verify the activities they describe, and these instances do falsify or verify that activity. The agent is less evident, and may need working out. Thus if De Gaulle, in mufti, falls into Gestapo hands, and under interrogation says "There is no such person as De Gaulle", that statement falsifies itself <u>for us</u>, who are primed on the true facts, but not for the interrogator. For him, the prisoner's identity has first to be revealed, before his statement can be seen as contradictory. And if in later years we see someone on television wearing Free French uniform, with a disgusted expression and a tallish cap, and saying "Moi, De Gaulle, I exist, I act, I make history ... ", this performance, which <u>if true</u> would be an instance of itself, will not convince us that it must be true, De Gaulle being God's gift to wooden-faced comedians.

Moving to the first person may appear to help. Surely if I say "I exist" I have verified my statement just by making it? The question of identification can hardly now arise. 'I' means the speaker, whoever he is or may pretend to be; and the remark must surely refer to him. Yet the statement does not instantiate itself (as does "English utterance in the present tense is in progress now"). Rather, my making it requires it to be true, just as for anything else I might describe and do, suiting the action to the word, e.g. "here I come".

A stat may confirm 'I exist', though not without some need for inference; it may be withdrawn from cavil by speaking it in soliloquoy, but only in the same old empty way and by appeal to the same old principle that actions need agents, that thoughts need thinkers to be thinking them.

*   *   *   *

The position now is this: the <u>Cogito</u> fails to prove to me that I exist, though the same logical relation shows why I had better not deny it, if I think I think. For such people, then, 'I think' is undeniable. Which is just what is conveyed by Hintikka's alternative line of thought.

Such 'undeniables' make up that wider range of arguably certain truths which, we said, Descartes proposed to admit by relaxing the metaphysical criterion (#5 above). Such truths might well be formed into a science:

> Transcendental Psychology is everything that one cannot deny about mental capacities short of disqualifying oneself as a being capable of finding out what is so about anything at all, let alone as a psychologist (Meynell 1980; cp Boyle + 1972).

Before considering such a system of thought we need to look further at the relation of presupposition, on which many proposed proofs of undeniability depend.

Note A . Are Syllogisms Circular?

The charge of presumptive circularity has been brought against syllogistic reasoning quite in general. Thus suppose I have watched many programmes described as comedies and found them unfunny, and one such comes on tonight, I shall not expect to be amused. This inference from my past unfortunate experience is far from conclusive, but by no means circular. But if someone says "All so-called comedies are unfunny therefore so will this one be", his inference is valid but may not satisfy us as a proof. For, we may ask, how can he know they are all unfunny except by watching all of them? In which case that general premiss cannot be known without the aid of the conclusion it was meant to prove (cp Mill II,ch iii; Stebbing 128).

Let us grant this major point: rules which can be known only by verifying all their instances are not to be used in proving any of those instances. That leaves us free to argue to an instance from rules which can be verified some other way; e.g. the rule that every triangle must have a mid-point. We can also argue from a rule less than completely verified; e.g. that bread nourishes, that fire burns, that sugar will dissolve in tea. Whatever convictions we may rightly hold on such matters, on the basis of man's extensive but still incomplete experience, such convictions may rightly be transferred by a valid argument to further, unexamined instances, without losing what force they may have or incurring a charge of circularity.

Mill's complaint does hold against some uses of some syllogisms of a certain type; for, indeed, you can't prove instances from rules they are needed to support.

Backward arguments from presupposition are objectionable in just the same way as the argument from previous unfunny comedies. The objection is, that one premiss cannot be sustained without appeal to the conclusion as already known. But the reason why is different. In the one case, it is claimed that the general unfunniness of so-called comedies could only be fully established by reviewing all the instances. In the other case, it is claimed that the propriety of saying "All John's children are in bed" can be established only by showing that John does have children. Claims like the first have been much debated. The second seems more evident.

Chapter Four

PRESUPPOSITION AND BACKWARD ARGUMENT

In a presumptively circular argument, like the <u>Cogito</u>, the premisses can be established only by appeal to the conclusion they were intended to enforce. Yet the same conclusion might still be shown undeniable-for-Smith, and by the very same argument. For if that argument is valid, it would be inconsistent to deny the conclusion and still assert the premisses. The statement exhibiting such inconsistency is true as a matter of logic, and needs no factual support. Smith can therefore be warned without circularity that if he says he thinks he had better not be denying he exists.

The <u>Cogito</u> is p-circular, so cannot prove its conclusion, but it can show that conclusion undeniable for those who continue to assert the premisses. Is this double-action common to all such backward arguments, or is it peculiar to this conundrum of Descartes?

p-circular arguments certainly form a more extended class. We shall study first those that move back from a statement presupposing so-and-so to so-and-so (the item presupposed). These backward arguments are p-circular <u>of necessity</u>. They have close links with the <u>Cogito</u>, and also with several transcendental deductions proposed by Kant.

15. REFEREES

Any argument from complex to constituent is potentially p-circular; for the complex could not be there, were the constituent not available, so you need the constituent first to make sure you do have the complex so as to start the inference back to the constituent again. On a desert island, then, you could never get into position to start arguing from ham and eggs to eggs.

But suppose you start off with ham-and-eggs, thoughtfully pre-wrapped by your friendly supermarket chain. Before undoing the packet you may reason "we have eggs", without logical vice or circularity. The inference is p-circular only if the package of premisses cannot be known without knowing the conclusion first. So the question is: Which complexes can be known without first knowing their constituents?

The statement "George hit Bill", if made, must be made by someone and to somebody. Without a receiver, no communication can occur; without a sender, the message will not even start. But something further is required, if information is to pass thereby from sender to recipient: both must have in mind the same two characters called 'George' and 'Bill', to refer the message to. Without such referees the message will be 'in the air': intelligible in a general way, but unapplied. To mark this further requirement we say the statement 'presupposes' George and Bill (cp Collingwood 21, Strawson _Theory_ 175).

There is nothing mystical or deep in this relationship. It just describes one requirement involved in 'referring to so-and-so'. Any reference requires a referrer and a referee, just as any knock-out requires a knocker-out and a knock-out-ee. As the action of referring normally takes place in speech, the action itself can be represented by quoting the words used in doing it. To keep this presented action distinct from the rest of the statement it is often best to put it in quotation marks.

On some accounts the statement "George hit Bill" does not presuppose Bill, but only George. The reason given is that the statement would merely be false, if Bill were not available, whereas

39

without George it is 'improper', neither true nor false. Of course this proposed convention has difficulties of its own. Consider

    A.   The King of France played chess with Eden
    B.   Eden played chess with the King of France

To the untutored eye A and B offer alternative descriptions of the same non-event; yet on the convention proposed A would be improper while B was only false (cp Donellan 1981).

    Such questions would clearly have to be decided, by reluctant fiat if by nothing else, in the course of constructing a logical calculus intended to cater for this new relationship. We have no such exalted aim. We shall therefore consider it only as found in and affecting ordinary arguments expressed in English words. Fortunately for us, most of the interesting points concern presupposed subjects like George, not presupposed objects, like Bill (cp Kempson 86).

    The referee required by a referential statement need not be a person. It may be a fact or event, an idea or a theory. Instead of a name we then find a phrase beginning 'that'. Thus

    S   The orbits of the planets round the sun are all elliptical

relies on a prior, factual point

    F   The planets do move in regular paths around the sun

If F were not so, S would not succeed in saying anything; for you can't describe the shape of the planets' orbits if the 'wandering' stars are not even orbiting (cp Hare 1964, Lloyd 1957).

16. ARGUING BACK

    Given some statement S which in this way presupposes or requires some factual item F we may say that S is 'improper' unless F is true. Thus the truth of F is a necessary condition for the 'propriety' of S (for there being something for S to be about).

IV.16 Arguing Back

This necessary condition can be made the basis of an inference:

S presupposes F
S is proper
    therefore F (is true)

Such a 'backward' inference is certainly valid, for S could not be proper unless F were true - that is part of the meaning of 'S presupposes F'. But we need to consider how such propriety is verified.

Suppose we found the statement S (about the planets) in a respected text-book of astronomy. We might take its truth for granted, and infer F from it. That inference would be sound, if we don't mind relying on authority. If we do mind, then the propriety of S will have to be specially verified - which cannot be done without appealing to the truth of F, thus making the inference p-circular.

The propriety of a statement is its having something to refer to or be about. This propriety can be confirmed by checking the truth of each of its presuppositions in the case of S, by verifying F. There seems to be no other way to confirm the propriety of S. We do very commonly take such things on trust, not only from text-books but in conversation and on reading notices; and if we proceed to inference on this basis our various conclusions would merit whatever trust we were rightly reposing in the premisses. But an inference to F can hardly be allowed, for if that is the point at question then we may not take it on authority, and must not proceed both to it and from it in an inference.

In this argument from presupposition the first premiss

    1. S presupposes F

shows that S is proper only if F is really the case, so that S can be <u>known</u> proper only by knowing F is true. Which is to say that the second premiss

    2. S is proper

cannot be known without the aid of the conclusion,

    3. F is true

IV.16 Arguing Back

This suggests a more general formulation of this objectionable type of argument. Where three propositions 1, 2, 3 are so constituted that if 1 is true then 2 cannot be known without the aid of 3, there the conclusion (3) cannot be properly proven on the basis of knowledge of the premisses (1, 2), even though it must be true when they are known.

An argument in this form can be found within the <u>Cogito</u>, for the thought 'I think' not only requires a thinker to be thinking it, but also presupposes an 'I' as referee. Now to infer the existence of that referee, from the given thought 'I think', one would need first of all to be sure of that thought's propriety. Many thoughts are improper, e.g. all present thoughts about the current King of France. To make sure that a thought is proper, we first have to check that the person or item referred to is available for reference. In the case of the <u>Cogito</u>, that means establishing the conclusion before even starting on the inference (cp Palmer 1981c).

17. LINGUISTIC ARGUMENT

Humpty Dumpty's view was obstructed, in a certain direction. This led him, one day, to wonder what proof there was for the existence of his legs. He was never one to take his stand on hearsay (cp Wittgenstein #429).

But you must have legs, said Alice. You need them to run with.

How do you know? I do go along quite quick, sometimes, but I might be flying or floating, like a duck or a bird.

Humpty Dumpty the Hovercraft, giggled Alice.

But Humpty began to go dark and swell with rage. She must think of something else, quick, for him to think about, before he burst. She remembered a topic dear to his heart:

It really depends on what you want the words to mean. If 'run' means 'move quickly' then runners won't require legs, and ships and bullets and bicycles will 'run'. But if 'run'

IV.17 Linguistic Argument

means 'go quickly on from one leg to the other' then bicycles don't run, strictly speaking, and whatever does run in the proper sense must be equipped with legs. So the question is, what do you mean by 'run'?

The question is, said Humpty grumpily, what sort of running do I do?

The world's roundest sceptic pondered a moment.

Here, give me a hand down off this wall. Quick now. We'll soon see what running really means ...

Famous last words. But Alice's quibble is significant. We do need to settle what our terms will mean, before starting on the argument. Even a good argument will only prove a conclusion in the sense its terms were bearing in the premises. And in this case the warning was well-placed. If 'run' means 'go along on legs, fast' then Humpty Dumpty cannot verify 'I run' while remaining doubtful of his legs. So a backward argument from motion cannot serve to establish his appendages: it is too circular for that.

* * * *

A backward argument, such as the Cogito, rests on an attempted reference. Some fact or individual is sufficiently indicated to the audience as object of the reference. The referrer then goes on to say something about that referee; but his remark cannot achieve truth, or even falsity, if its referee is not available for reference. So if the remark is true then the reference must have been proper, i.e. the referee was available for reference. Truth demands Propriety. It is on this principle that backward inference depends. It would work very well, if only that Truth could be established while that Propriety remains in doubt.

Not every reference, however, is literally meant. In "It's raining" the 'it' needs now no referee other than the rain. 'Sundown' marks only a change from day towards night, and need not betoken belief in a downward motion of the sun. These turns of phrase are now metaphorical; and we shall not label the statements which contain them improper, on failing to find referees for them literally as

43

IV.17 Linguistic Argument

described. So we had better not base any backward arguments on them.

Could it be, then, that 'I think' is only a traditional personalized turn of phrase for certain mental processes? How much scientific weight ought we to place on a customary one-letter word? Granted that <u>in our language</u> thoughts are thought to need thinkers, can we safely transfer that necessity from language to reality? These queries suggest that every backward argument is really a linguistic inference-ticket, and valid only on our local language-railway (cp Mundle 126).

Every stated inference depends on its terms continuing to bear the sense they started with. It also presumes a more general background of linguistic agreement among the arguers (cp #5 above). Every argument, indeed every statement is linguistically dependent in this minimal way. Backward arguments, however, have a stronger dependence on how we take their terms. We need to decide at the outset whether the referring phrase is to be taken literally, or not.

If some items of speech are admitted metaphorical no backward argument can be relied on by simply assuming that the reference in the premisses is literal. We must first show it to be literal, and then begin the argument. But this means showing that certain facts are thus and so: how else could one show that the expression used for those facts is literally appropriate? For example, before arguing from 'she runs' to some real 'she' we must first investigate that action to make sure that the subject in our description was literally meant. That is, we must first show that actions need agents, in the real world, in order to show that the way verbs cry out for subjects, in our language, is appropriate and literally meant, not just an accident of our historically conditioned local form of speech (cp Yarvin 1977, Ward 1970).

So even if a backward inference were reliable as inference, it would only indicate a linguistic necessity, which might be a mere accident, or just a metaphor. To carry full conviction the inference must still rely on the material principle that actions need real live personal agents. Thus while 'I think' does as a matter of grammar presuppose an 'I', thinking may or may not require a thinker, in

IV.17 Linguistic Argument

reality. We may of course be personally convinced that actions need agents, in the world, but we can't prove this from the fact that verbs of action need subjects which are personal.

At best, a backward argument will indicate a linguistic link deserving further attention as perhaps representing a real linkage on which we could depend; e.g. 'I think's presupposing 'I' does suggest that thoughts need thinkers, a material point which must then be somehow settled on its own. Thus when Buddhists are found denying the Self any ultimate reality we may not refute them just by reference to the conjugation of the English verb, but we may take that as a pointer to certain fleeting phenomena in this ambiguous world of ours, phenomena which the Buddhist also admits and which we find incompatible with an impersonal analysis.

If 'thoughts need thinkers' is established to our full satisfaction now and evermore, then we may argue on in either material or linguistic mode:

(M) 'I think' must be true if said, so I exist

(L) 'I think' being true must be properly said, so I exist

Both inferences are p-circular, for you cannot confirm that you think, nor display the propriety of saying so, without referring to the 'I' which the argument was meant to prove. In refutation, however, either line of inference can be deployed: to show any Smith who says he thinks why not to deny that he exists.

18. COUNTERING A DOUBT

All backward arguments are bound to be p-circular, so cannot prove their conclusions. But when people holding certain views try to deny those conclusions they can be refuted by means of backward inference.

This distinction between refutation and proof may become clearer if we briefly review the various ways of countering a doubt by means of argument.

IV.18 Countering a Doubt

Imagine once more that familiar dramatic nobody, the out-and-out sceptic. His profession is to achieve ignorance, established defensible armour-plated ignorance, of what everybody knows. Round he goes smashing up all the fabric of belief. Our republic of letters has need of some gallant defenders to repulse this dangerous attack. Fortunately for us, there are several different lines of defence that they can man:

A. Provide Better Premisses Doubts about the abominable snowman could of course be countered by producing one. In this game facts are trumps. But in most disputed cases the item disputed is not one we could display. The astrologer cannot show us cases of stellar influence, but can only claim that conjunctions of supernal and terrestrial events go far beyond coincidence. The scientist also cannot show us a magnet pulling iron, nor indeed gravity pulling apples, or even fire making kettles boil. He can only claim that those repeated conjunctions go far beyond coincidence.

If such links are questioned, the assertor may collect more instances of the conjunction (cases of Falling Apple) or look around for similar phenomena (Evidence of Downward Tendency in Cricket Balls). Back-up of this sort makes up much of everyday research in science.

Now the question was: Do such conjunctions constitute a link? That cannot be answered just by finding more of them. But finding more instances would increase the 'coincidence' in supposing each conjunction happened independently.

B. Improve the Proof Where the assertor based his assertion on an inference he can try to display that inference more clearly, in response to questioning, or to indicate its relation to other modes of argument already accepted as reliable. Such studies form part of logic, and the bulk of philosophy of science.

*   *   *   *

In these two cases the assertor counters a doubt by trying to strengthen his assertion. So he should end up with a positive case which is stronger at just those points where the sceptic has pointed out the weaknesses.

IV.18 Countering a Doubt

C. Disable the Disproof   A sceptical attack consists of reasoning, which can in its turn be attacked by further reasoning. Here the roles are confusingly reversed, the assertor playing sceptic to the sceptic's assertions. The sceptic must have started from some premisses. Perhaps these can be rejected as evidently false, or as not knowably true, or as spurious or meaningless. Or the sceptic's reasoning may be rejected by comparison with standard types already recognized as unreliable (a widely accepted move, though unreliable). These negative reactions correspond to the two types A,B, of positive reply.

*   *   *   *

A positive reply, A or B, may not silence the sceptic, who can continue to allege coincidence. A successful negative reply, C, should at least put a stop to that particular sceptical argument, but it does not advance matters for the audience. For an attack disabled leaves the position attacked just as sound or unsound as it was before. Showing the sceptic wrong does not show his opponent to be right.

D. Show denial incoherent   An assertor under attack may say the sceptic's attack is out of place, since his finding things so dubious is not compatible with their really being so. Here the sceptic's denial is understood, well enough to see its incoherence and infer that such denial has to be denied. Descartes founded his system on such an indirect inference-from-doubt, and Kant's transcendental deductions develop a similar line of reasoning.

*   *   *   *

We shall not be concerned, in this book, with improvements in direct positive proof of items which the sceptic doubts; with dredging up a coelocanth or climbing Ararat to find the Ark (A). Nor shall we be systematizing the syllogism or devising a calculus of probability (B). Nor shall we spend time on direct rebuttals (C), in which the assertor questions the sceptic's starting-point or detects fallacy within his reasoning. Our concern is entirely with <u>indirect</u> refutations (D), which

47

IV.18 Countering a Doubt

profess to show by argument that certain argued doubts are untenable, because unstatable.

Where this incoherence or inconsistency is not immediately obvious it will need to be deduced and displayed in a lemma or side-proof. Moreover the refutation as a whole is indirect in character: it makes us abandon an idea by showing its consequences to be unacceptable. Such an indirect refutation can thus be mistaken for a new and positive (but indirect) proof of the item under sceptical attack.

An indirect proof compels us to accept some disputed item, D, by showing that conflicting consequences (C, not-C) would flow from its contradictory, not-D. Not-D must be false, then, therefore D is true (assuming it must be either true or false, cp Haack 66f). In an indirect refutation, the item under debate is shown (by a proof, perhaps) to conflict with conditions involved in our debating it. Here again a denial leads to a conflict, but the conflict is not due to the item denied (as with not-D) but is generated <u>by our denying it</u>. To remove this conflict we need not contradict the denial, but only cease from making it. There is thus an important difference between proving something to be true and showing it to be undeniable.

Note B . Arguments ad hominem

Those who say transcendental arguments only work <u>ad hominem</u> may be casting fresh darkness on the topic, by use of this uncertain term.

In modern logic-books it usually refers to personal attacks intended to discredit an opponent rather than confront his argument. For Locke it meant pressing someone "with consequences drawn from his own principles and concessions" (<u>Essay</u> IV xx 21); presumably, his <u>other</u> known principles, for any arguer may be pressed with what he just conceded in that very argument. Locke means attacking Smith's present doctrine, D, for inconsistency with Smith's earlier pronouncements, A, B, C. And of course this objection is 'personal' to Smith, or at least to those who share Smith's doctrines A,B,C (cp Hamblin 160, Copi 100).

Either way, a 'personal' argument is not any particular type of inference or fallacy, but a sort of debating move, which is quite effective and proper in certain circumstances. Such a move can however be used only against Smith, and like-minded persons. It does not by itself refute his doctrine, D, or even the argument he used for it. At best, an ad hominem reply shows that Smith has no business to be advancing D.

A transcendental argument is partly similar to such 'personal' refutations. They discredit Smith's doctrine, D, by reference to his earlier theories, A, B, C. It contrasts Brown's explicit present thesis, T, with P, the position he occupies while propounding it. Brown may not be aware of P, or he may have forgotten it, but he does occupy it - for T can only be propounded by some such occupant.

This objection is, in its way, 'personal' to Brown. It applies to anyone in his position: "We don't object to what you are saying but to someone in your position saying it".

We didn't mind Smith saying D, only his saying-D-while-still-asserting-A, B, C. So Smith can avoid our objection by dropping any one of them. In the transcendental case, Brown can avoid our objection (and continue propounding T) only by abandoning his position P, i.e. by stopping what he is doing, e.g. propounding-a-thesis. For Brown, this evasive action is a more serious affair (cp Hinman 1982).

Chapter Five

KANT'S VINDICATION OF GEOMETRY

An argument back to a presupposed item from the propriety of the statement presupposing it is bound to be p-circular, as the alleged propriety consists simply in that item being available for reference. Thus one premiss declares that the other can only be established by means of the conclusion those premisses were supposed to be establishing.

Such an argument in any case depends on the items being <u>literally</u> presupposed; as 'Swan Upping' does refer to a real movement up of swans, but 'sundown' no longer implies any motion of the sun. To make sure an item is literally meant we must consider <u>it</u>, e.g. swans. If we can do that, they need not be inferred. If we can't, any inference back to them will be dubious until its conclusion has been reached. Here the p-circular argument grows another loop.

Arguments of this backward, presuppositional variety play an important part in the philosophy of Kant.

19. A SCIENCE OF PHENOMENA

Kant's new 'critical' philosophy is billed to refute scepticism and idealism, not to mention materialism, fatalism, atheism, free-thinking, fanaticism and superstition (B xxxiv), by showing how we can achieve real knowledge of our world. Scepticism is "the profession and science of ignorance, by which all knowledge would be undermined, leaving nothing reliable and nothing safe"(B 451). The typical and "most ingenious" sceptic was Hume, who saw that causal connections

V.19 A Science of Phenomena

are never observed and never proved, and inferred that we must be inventing them (B 792f).

The view that things are not real, or may not be, is briskly dismissed under the name 'idealism', quite late on in the book (B 274). Kant's main target is not this outright denial of external things, but doubts as to whether connections and processes are knowable. How do we know that every event is caused? Some say that we just do know, and that is that. It is this 'dogmatic' response, Kant says, that turns men into sceptics, though of course that experience soon turns them back into dogmatists again (B 23).

Scepticism is thus a resting-place for human reason, where it can reflect upon its dogmatic wanderings and make survey of the region in which it finds itself, so that for the future it may be able to choose its path with more certainty. But it is no dwelling-place for permanent settlement (B 789).

If our science does rely on unobserved connections and constructions then we need to see how these come in. Without them, science would collapse: yet we cannot just take them as 'given' and retain our scientific self-respect (A xi).

Kant's theory is that the structural aspects of experience are indeed contributed by us, and that we therefore know these structures 'inside out', and can be sure that they apply to everything we do or could experience. This explains why we know some things 'in advance': e.g. we know what to expect if a hole is dug beneath the house, and we know it without trying first, 'in advance' (B 2).

For Hume, causal connections are fictional; for Kant, they are contributed by us, along with several other fundamental and structural ideas. For Hume, ideas made up and contributed by us will not convey the truth of things: if fictional, not factual. For Kant, we can be sure of understanding only the ideas we put in: scientific insight comprehends just the items contributed by us. So has Kant refuted Hume, or just recited his scepticism back to front, to make it sound less frightening?

V.19 A Science of Phenomena

Perception, for Hume, is passive: we look at the world and just drink in how things really are. For Kant, it has an active element: perception consists of the given-as-structured-by-us-in-perceiving-it. The sciences he offers to explain provide knowledge of this contributed, structural element. The other, given element will still be given, as before; but not on its own, neat and unstructured. So we cannot tell what that neat, unstructured given would be like if no-one were perceiving it.

We never had and never could have a science of how things _really_ are, on their own, unperceived-by-us. (No loss.) But we do have true and guaranteed sciences of the structural aspects of our perceptions, the framework of our world. (We had these sciences before, but no-one had realized just how we could be having them.) Of the given as structured in that world we can have perceptions, and so can learn to find our way about. (No change: detailed physical enquiry must remain empirical.)

It may be felt that this theory is needlessly sceptical: sceptical in saying that we can't tell what things are really like, apart from our perceiving them (permanent pink spectacles would discolour everything); needlessly so, as in that case we could never be sure that things are really different from their appearances to us (maybe the world _is_ just that shade of pink). This objection rests on the false analogy with spectacles, which can be taken off, so that colours and shapes can be seen as 'distorted' from those seen separately by the naked eye. But the elements Kant says we contribute are structural, e.g. spatial arrangement. What would it mean to know non-spatially that which our perception organizes spatially? It seems like trying to check on a jig-saw picture by inspecting the pieces jumbled in the box (cp Allison 1974).

Let us try another analogy, not available to Kant. A television picture is, no doubt, produced and assembled by the receiver in our home. We may never go to the studios to see what the people shown on our screen are 'really' like. Lacking such evidence, we have to allow that they may be very different, when untelevised: that the staging and transmission and reproduction processes _may_ regularly distort some qualities they really have (e.g. present all colours as just black-and-white) and impose others which they never had (all people and situations same-sized to a fifty-centimetre square). But then, for all we know, those actors and stage-sets may have just those qualities which we thought were being contributed by our little box.

Kant suggests that Reality is non-spatial and non-temporal, and that our glimpses of it get organized spatially and temporally, by us, while having them. So he says we cannot know what Things are really like. Fair enough, in the sense that you cannot <u>know</u> what someone is really like just by looking <u>at</u> a photograph. That doesn't stop the photograph giving you quite a good idea. One should not infer that the subject photographed, George-in-himself, is therefore quite unknowable.

Kant's main point remains: that all we can know are things-as-observed: phenomena.

20. CONTRIBUTED IDEAS

Our ideas presumably either come to us from without, or have their origin within; and these latter must either be our own work or else have been with us all along. As such divisions (into X and non-X) are sure to leave nothing out and to count nothing twice, a double dichotomy should give a satisfactory listing of ideas: adventitious, fictitious and innate (Descartes <u>Meditations</u> 3). But dividing will not by itself tell <u>us which</u> divisions are actually occupied, or what their occupants are worth.

For Locke and his followers, no ideas were innate. All our knowledge, then, should be traceable to information acquired during life (home-made ideas being disregarded as merely fictional). We gather information bit by bit, like a series of snapshots, and from these separate and successive items no reliable general conclusions can be drawn. No amount of sunbathing can show that <u>tomorrow's</u> sun, if it shines, will make us warm. <u>At most we</u> can say "It always has, so far"(B 3f).

No observational science, then, can be quite reliable and general. We 'live and learn', no doubt, but shall never live to learn that <u>every</u> triangle has a mid-point. Yet our geometry <u>makes</u> just such claims. Such a science cannot be observational.

V.20 Contributed Ideas

There is a further difficulty in making science empirical. Natural science deals largely with connections, with links inferred, but not observed, between events. We see the sun shining. We notice a stone getting warm, and say "the sun warms the stone" - going beyond what we actually observed. That extra link is contributed by us.

Now suppose one managed to frame such fictional connections into a proper-looking 'science'. What would it be a science of? Not of things and their natures, but only of our imaginative practices.

This inference of Hume's was turned around by Kant. A science describing our contributions to experience should at least be fully knowable, as we shall regularly contribute to experience just those elements that it describes. It is by this revolution of perspective that a body of disconnected particular information can become a real universal Science: first mathematics, then mechanics and now chemistry have gone Copernican, making the observer part of the scene observed, so that his objects are precisely what he sees in them.

This striking suggestion contained one element that was traditional: our ideas may or may not be 'true' to anything outside, but at least we do have them and must know precisely what they are (Descartes Meditations 3). On the qualities and relations of Smith's ideas A and B, Smith is the only and the best authority. Mathematics, then, which involves comparing and relating clear and definite ideas, is a genuine science; and morality too might become one, if the definitions were tidied up a bit (Locke IV.iii.#18).

On this view geometry catalogues the consequences of certain definitions (of circle, triangle etc) agreed on at the start. The proofs just analyse the structure and relations of the concepts there defined. If Smith agrees to Brown's definition of a triangle, that shows he shares the same idea, and the whole system follows from these agreements, by a process of analysis (cp Wood 1962).

Kant however denied that geometry is just analysis:

54

Give a philosopher the idea of a triangle and let him discover philosophically what its angles add up to. All he has is the idea of a three-cornered figure bounded by three staight lines. Meditation on this will never reveal anything. Analysing and clarifying <u>corner</u>, <u>straight line</u>, and <u>three</u> will not lead to other properties not contained in those ideas. Now let a geometer try. He at once constructs a triangle. Knowing that the adjacent angles at one point on a straight line all together equal two right angles, he extends one side of his triangle, and thus gets two adjacent angles summing to two right angles. He then divides the external angle by a line parallel to the opposite side ... Guided by intuition all the way he thus achieves, by a chain of inferences, a solution both evident and fully general (B 744f; cp Oguah 1980).

Proof is still personal, on this account, but does not result from arbitrary choice. We cannot choose what to see, if we open our eyes: nor can we decide what relations to discover in a diagram. Mathematical facts are facts about something contributed by us, that is why they can be known to us with certainty; but still, they are given and objective facts, not invented but discovered in that medium. Though not merely analytic, geometry is still certain, being prior to experience. Only 'inside information' could give us such synthetic yet 'a priori' knowledge about things.

21. CONSTRUCTION

Geometrical facts are 'just-seen' (intuited), and they are facts about something (Space) contributed by us. But they do not come easily or at once, just by a little look inside.

Such introspection, Kant argued, would be no more reliable than our observations of the outside world. What we finally perceive, in both cases, is a composite: given fact <u>plus</u> perceptual ordering <u>equals</u> item-as-perceived (B 153). Mere observations, then, of phenomena internal to ourselves would remain separate and serial as outer observations do, and could not by themselves constitute a science.

V.21 Construction

Just how, then, can a science result from Space being our contribution to phenomena? Kant says this comes by 'construction of concepts' - an unilluminating phrase. In modern parlance, 'construction' refers to extra lines put into a diagram to assist the proof. For Kant, the whole diagram has this abstract and arbitrary status: it is something we think up and then put in front of ourselves to think about (cp Hintikka 1969a). The diagram we draw need not derive from any particular experience, but is created imaginatively 'in advance' (B 741f). Deduction and discovery are then required; the hard work and luck every schoolboy knows geometry to be. For

> you didn't just have to trace out what you could see in the triangle, or in your idea of it, and just learn off its properties from that. You had to bring out what you yourself had thought into it, conceptually, in advance, by presenting it in a diagram (B xii, cp 762).

You think of a triangle. You draw it. You discover its properties; e.g. it must have a midpoint. Although discovered in an individual diagram, this property seems general, as the diagram did not specify the actual measurements of the angles or the sides:

> we attend only to the business of presenting the idea in a diagram, and disregard these peculiarities, which make no difference to the concept 'triangle'(B 742).

This explains, with no great novelty, how one particular diagram with all its individual peculiarities could serve in proof of a theorem about many very different triangles.

We could also ask: Why should such properties recur at all? Why should the next bit of Space display the same version of triangularity? We need to be sure that all parts of Space are uniform; and we can be sure of this only if Space is contributed by us. Geometry is a science for us because we are just reading off Nature what we first read into it (cp B xviii). The circle, i.e. all the points at the same distance from one point, is just <u>not there</u> till drawn (Letter to Herz, 26 May 1789).

V.21 Construction

There is a further question here, less evident to Kant. Why should all of us read into Nature just the same geometry? Can I rely on you to contribute to your perceptual Space just those structural properties that I do to mine? Confronted with a pyramid, can we be sure its builders also saw it as triangular? This rather basic point cannot be settled, it seems, by agreement in verbal description, or in pictorial representation - or even by the pyramid itself. Neither my experience, nor yours on the same occasion, can guarantee that the experiences we are having are the same.

Once again, the solution lies in the fact of our shared geometry. We may not know for certain how the Pharaohs saw the pyramids, but we do know what Euclid said about such shapes. We can read him with understanding and carry out his proofs, so we must share the same space to be arguing about.

So we share a Space with Euclid. Why must it be 'ours' (and 'his')? What evidence has Kant for this unconscious salting of the mine to produce nuggets of geometry? Simply that he can see no other way for us to have a real science. Transcendental Idealism is our only hope of acquiring synthetic a priori truth.

22. STARTING FROM SCIENCE

Kant has justified geometry, like this:

A. The theorems of a genuine science must be certain and necessary. Observational generalizations cannot be certain or necessary. So a genuine science cannot be purely observational.

B. Geometry is a genuine science. So geometry cannot be purely observational.

C. Informative certainty can be had only about items contributed by us. Geometry, being a genuine science, offers informative certainties. So geometry is about something contributed by us (Space).

57

D. The geometer can be seen at work providing himself with these objective-yet-contributed-discoveries, whenever he draws and thinks about a diagram ('construction').

  *   *   *   *

Similar reasoning is applied to Time and to the pure science of motion (dynamics, minus those parts that refer to weight: see below Note C to #24). We do have such a science, its theorems are necessary and known with certainty, it can't be observational, so it must relate to a structure contributed by us in organizing our perceptions of phenomena.

As the arguments on Time run parallel, but are stated much more sketchily, we shall concentrate on Space.

  *   *   *   *

These arguments look valid. IF science must be certain and universal, to be science, and IF we do possess a science of geometry, THEN geometry must be about something contributed by us, IF certain and universal theorems can be reached only in that way.

We may of course grant the reasoning and reject the premisses. And the last 'if' does seem quite dubious. How could one show that a certain but informative geometry cannot be achieved in any other way? (Körner 1967). The negative would be difficult to prove, but the same point can be made as a challenge: Show me another way to acquire such geometry. This challenge, issued in 1781, has not yet been met.

It may also be questioned whether such geometry can be obtained, as Kant says, by 'construction of concepts'. His reasoning here depends heavily on metaphors: we 'put in' spatial properties while perceiving things, so we can 'take them out again' - like a suitcase from a cloakroom on the railway. Space is 'our contribution' so we know all about it - as a part-author knows his contribution to a book (cp Hintikka 1973). Such allusions can indeed suggest lines of enquiry, but they do not constitute an argument.

V.22 Starting from Science

Kant's reasoning, if compelling, would show his conclusion <u>as reliable as</u> his premisses - providing these <u>do not in their</u> turn rely on his conclusion for support. To check this point, we had better condense the argument a bit:

1. Geometry can be a genuine science only if Space is contributed by us
2. Geometry is a genuine science

so 3. Space is contributed by us.

In following this argument we would need to make sure of the authentic nature of the alleged science of geometry (2), while still trying to ascertain (3) whether Space is contributed by us. But premiss 1 says that 2 depends on 3. Now to base a proof of 3 on 1 and 2 you would need to make sure of them independently of 3. If 3 is needed first, to make 2 available, the argument is circular.

One may of course <u>say</u> that 2 is available to us independently of 3. <u>If</u> one has it on the very best authority that Euclid's geometry is a genuine science - e.g. one remembers being Euclid, in a previous life, and achieving it - one might well feel able to rely on this science as an independent given fact, irrespective of the condition attached thereto in Premiss 1. Anyone in this happy position can discover by Kant's argument that Space is transcendentally ideal. But Critical philosophers, even if re-incarnated, can hardly be allowed to take their previous discoveries on trust.

It does appear odd, in an argument about the nature and extent of science, to start out from this or that so-called science as a given fact. How can we say dogmatically that they <u>are</u> sciences, in the strict sense, while we are still discussing the data which they would be about?

One reason why it seems odd is that we are used to a 'foundational' approach: superstructures are to be justified by reference to their basic uncontroversial elements. Which is alright, if you really have those elements. Thus Locke sets out from the simple ideas each of us can pick up in the world, to see how our knowledge could all be built up from them; and he never gets to chemistry. His sceptical conclusion, that we cannot know the real properties of things, does follow from his atomic-observation starting-point. But it invites the

59

reply that some chemistry is actually known, whereas his psychological atomism is largely fictional. In terms of comparative assurance, then, the fact of science may be a better starting-point. No doubt the basic original ideas, if we do have them, are more ultimately reliable. But our account of how we acquire those ideas must come first, in the order of our coming-to-know. In reaching that account it is not silly to take some actual sciences as given facts (cp Bernsen 24).

Besides accepting the fact of sciences - that people do <u>know</u> this and that about stars and triangles - Kant also accepts a traditional view of the structure needed for those sciences. They must be deductive systems, theorems proved from previous theorems and so on back to a few fundamental axioms accepted as self-evident. This theory of science suggests that knowledge must always be completely general - <u>every</u> triangle <u>everywhere</u> and <u>everywhen</u> is X and Y - and it is this demand for generality that our atomized sensory information cannot satisfy.

That science is deductive in structure would have seemed to Kant a simple given fact. The only studies then accepted as successful sciences were regularly presented as networks of inter-supporting theorems, that format alone being thought scientifically respectable.

Deducing theorems in a system shows them to be as reliable as the axioms or principles we deduce them from. So if the theorems are to be proved absolutely true, the axioms will have to be known to be so, first. But they cannot be known so by any reference to theorems within that system: deduction is a way of getting truth and certainty to flow down from the origins. Everything else in the system gets its truth and certainty from the axioms, so they can't depend on anything else in the system, on pain of circularity. Thus if geometry is a deductive system then the geometrical axioms either have no further warranty but are, we hope, 'self-evident', or else their guarantee must come from outside the system, and be non-geometrical. Proving them geometrically would just extend the system backwards to a different set of axioms, about which the same problem would arise (cp Nelson II.15f).

A certain picture of the sciences has been built up from this view. There are several

V.22 Starting from Science

systematic (deductive) sciences, each with its own set of principles: geometry, dynamics, physics, biology perhaps, one day even history ... Since each needs its own set of principles, and none can possibly provide its own, there must be some separate super-science whose job it is to manufacture and distribute ready-wrapped axiom-sets, stamped and 'guaranteed reliable'. Metaphysics is that super-science (cf Aristotle 55,122).

This remarkable inference is by now so familiar, in Introductions to Philosophy, that it is easy to overlook its logical character. Perhaps a parallel will help: "round sugarcubes are not available at the grocer's so they must be on sale at the Post Office".

Kant often speaks as though his Transcendental theory were a super-science turning out proofs for the axioms of each and every science. At other times his claim is more modest: to describe a human condition in which humans could find they know such principles. The Aesthetic conforms to this latter, modest programme. The Analytic of Principles looks more like the former. The Transcendental Deduction can be taken either way (cp Bubner 1975).

The claim that we do know something is not unreasonable, even at the start. The claim that what we know must be necessary and general, deductive in structure yet applied to real things, is a bigger claim - but of course a better send-off for a Transcendentalist.

23. DID KANT ARGUE BACK?

It is not silly to find something you know and ask how you could be knowing it. But this 'self-referential' or reflexive line of thought is out of place for proving general facts about the process of human knowledge, facts which then help to decide what sorts of thing are known. For that puts into question again the 'knowledge' accepted at the outset as reliable (Bubner 1975, Rorty 1977).

It may be said that the argument back from the fact of science was not needed to prove Kant's novel theory, but only to help explain it, in the nursery version Prolegomena (1783). That would be a great relief, if true, but ought not to be accepted just

V.23 Did Kant argue back?

because we wish it were. To settle the point, some study of textual details is required (cp Baum 1977).

<u>Prolegomena</u> does explain, more than once, why it was needed to explain what the Critique had just explained at length (in 1781). <u>Prolegomena</u> is just an outline, a sketch-plan of results achieved, without the arguments (Preface, Appendix). This is a fair description of the latter part of the book (#24f), which just summarizes the Principles, the Dialectic and the Method. This outline, moreover, is to be arranged "according to the analytic method", whereas the Critique itself was 'synthetic' in approach. This contrast may suit the first two-fifths of the book, which partly re-argue the themes of Introduction, Aesthetic and Deduction. But it is far from obvious what the contrast would involve.

Synthesis means putting together: literally assembling real parts, or figuratively 'putting two and two together', moving onward from the reason to the consequence. Analysis means taking to bits: either real bits, or contributing reasons analyzed out from the resulting consequence (<u>Dissertation</u> #1). In working a problem, both methods might be used: thus if asked to bisect a line at right angles one might work up from the given line 'synthetically', then imagine the result achieved and work back from there, hoping stalactite will reach down as far as stalagmite is reaching up, to knit them together in one continuous proof (cp Robinson 1936). Now <u>Prolegomena</u> does start 'analytically' from our knowing some synthetic a priori truths, i.e. from the fact of science. Kant adds that a proposition is synthetic if it adds to the subject-idea, analytic otherwise; analytic <u>method</u> need not involve such analytic <u>propositions</u>, and could well be called 'regressive' to avoid this confusion (P #5).

This distinction of method is not drawn in the Critique (A), not even in the "Method". In the second edition it appears in asides, without explanation: the analytic approach is <u>a posteriori</u> (B 115 - because accepting science as a fact?), the synthetic approach combines concepts to arrive at theorems (B 395n, 416). We cannot discover from these casual remarks which way Kant thought he was arguing in other and more fundamental segments of his theory. "Perhaps the most difficult thing about Kant's theory of geometry is distinguishing between

V.23 Did Kant argue back?

the premises and the conclusions'(Brittan 81).

The Aesthetic offers reasons for supposing that Space and Time are somehow given in advance (A 23f,30f), inferring that they are "two sources of knowledge, from which bodies of a priori synthetic knowledge can be derived"(A 38). Were Space and Time not thus prior to phenomena, geometry and dynamics could not achieve their universal certainty (A 24,31). Indeed, if Space and Time were "in themselves objective" then seeing that "the propositions of geometry are synthetic a priori, and are known with apodeictic certainty, I raise the question, whence do you obtain such propositions?" and the only answer is to grant that Space and Time are subjective conditions after all (A 46f).

<u>Prolegomena</u> develops this argument from the fact of science: "certain pure synthetic knowledge a priori is real and given, namely pure mathematics and pure natural science"(P #4). By enquiring how such sciences, which are real, are 'possible', Kant deduces that Space is contributed by us, and that we apply unifying concepts or categories to make the resulting phenomena up into an intelligible world.

In the second edition of the Critique the argument that actual sciences must be possible is added to the Introduction (B 20). In the Aesthetic the reasons for supposing Space and Time given-in-advance are marked off (as 'Metaphysical Exposition') from a partly new 'Transcendental Exposition'. which is to provide an "explanation of a concept, as a principle from which the possibility of other a priori synthetic knowledge can be understood". In fact, it presents the argument from the fact of science (A 24,cp B 40f; A 31/B 47f).

In all these passages the same three propositions appear:

  S The science of geometry is possible if and only if Space is contributed by us.
  C Space is contributed by us.
  G We do have a science of geometry.

But these propositions are combined to form two quite different arguments. In the Critique Kant first produces reasons for believing C, then uses the 'if'-bit of S to establish G. Later on, using the 'only-if', he argues back from G to C.

V.23 Did Kant argue back?

Prolegomena develops this backward argument from the fact of science, which might well be called 'analytic', as moving from given knowledge back to the enabling conditions revealed by analysis. This backward argument is then inserted at several points in the Critique (second edition), under a new name which links it with the Deduction of the Categories and with Kant's overall conception of his work.

The Analytic provides a 'Metaphysical Deduction' of the Categories as unitive functions like those found in judgments, to show their 'a priori origin' (A 67f, cp B 159, P #21f). There is, however, within the Transcendental Deduction a considerable section to show how perceived items are put together into objects, and in just what way a perceiver is needed, to be doing this (A 92 - 114, cp B 129 - 142). This material is not found in Prolegomena, and could well be called 'synthetic', since it starts from the supposed elements of perception and proceeds by several syntheses towards knowledge or 'Experience'.

In contrasting 'synthetic' Critique with 'analytic' Prolegomena Kant may have been pointing to the backward movement of the argument from the fact of science, or to the constructive character of parts of the Deduction of the Categories; or both. In any case it seems that the backward line of argument became central to his scheme of thought regarding Space and Time.

An argument from science may add persuasion at this point. Had Kant been arguing not from but to a science of geometry, we could reasonably expect to find two further arguments in the Critique: first, to show that Space is indeed contributed by us, some argument based on facts other than the allegedly scientific status of geometry; second, deductions to establish the axioms of geometry (such as are offered for physics, in the Analogies). But the Critique provides no deductions of geometrical axioms; and the Metaphysical Exposition of Space (B 37f) is strikingly feeble as argument, though raising some interesting points - of a sort that Smith might think should come in handy for converting Robinson.

The forward argument has obvious weaknesses. It is not very clear how contributed-Space makes possible a science of geometry. The polemic against

V.23 Did Kant argue back?

Newton and Leibniz (A 23f) is far from compelling; in any case showing their theeories wrong would not show Kant's theory right, unless we knew in advance that no others were available. The backward argument by contrast is clear and valid. No wonder Kant moved across to it.

In sum: certain parts of the Critique (Metaphysical Exposition; Transcendental Deduction, first part) do not fall under our analysis, since they follow a different line of argument (cp Guyer 1982). The major fact remains that 'backward' argument from the fact of science does occur, irreplaceably, in both Critique and Prolegomena; and that this argument suffers from presumptive circularity.

24. REFUTING CERTAIN SETS OF VIEWS

A p-circular argument is incompetent as proof, for its conclusion is needed at the start, to bolster up the premisses. Such an argument may however indicate a certain logical relation between its conclusion and its premisses, which prohibits us from denying it while accepting them. To show this relation we replace the conclusion by its negation (marked with an asterisk):

1. Geometry can be a genuine science only if Space is contributed by us.
2. Geometry is a genuine science.
*3 Space is not contributed by us.

The original argument (1, 2 so 3), being valid, shows that this set of opinions (1, 2, *3) is inconsistent, that they cannot all be jointly true. And we can see this complicated fact of logical relationship without deciding which one of them is true. One of them must go - if you want to keep the other two. This result is not vitiated by circularity.

This inconsistent triad (1, 2, *3) can be deployed in refutations, in three different ways - depending which two items the victim may decide to 'keep':

Refutation I: if keeping 1 and 2, abandon *3.
   Those who hold with Kant that Geometry is given as a science, which it could not be

65

V.24 Refuting certain sets of views

unless Space were contributed by us, must not also assert that Space is an external, observable Reality. This does not prove that Transcendental Idealism is true, but does show it as the only refuge for those believing 1 and 2.

A refutation puts a price-tag on a certain set of views: if you want to go on believing A and B, consistency requires you to accept C or abandon D. The price for believing 1 and 2, it seems, is that Space be subjective. If we find that price too high, then something else will have to go. Kant did not envisage this outcome, but it was an important result of his system of philosophy.

<u>Refutation II</u>: keep 2 and *3, abandon 1.
Geometry is a genuine science, about real external things. This requires us to deny that a genuine science must be about items contributed by us.

The view of science as a deductive system of universal truths about real objects was in fact modelled on geometry, 'the exemplar and medium of all evidence in the other sciences'(<u>Dissertation</u> #15). Kant accepted this traditional view with one qualification: that the only objects accessible to us were partly-contributed 'phenomena'. Other modifications of the traditional view are also possible, but were not investigated by Kant. For example, one might emphasise the factual aspect but relax the 'certain and universal' claim: empirical inductive science would fit this bill. Or one might deny that 'inside information' <u>must</u> be more reliable, and seek certainty in a fully explicit and testable presentation, independent of each individual geometer.

<u>Refutation III</u>: keep *3 and 1, abandon 2.
A genuine science of geometry would require a Space contributed by us, which it isn't, so we cannot be having a genuine science of geometry, not in Kant's sense, anyway (cp B 64,274).

Of course we may have some other sort. For example, we may have a deductive system of geometrical-sounding theorems, derived from some

V.24 Refuting certain sets of views

arbitrary set of initial axioms carefully so chosen that real spatial facts are quite often found to coincide with the theorems derived (cp Strawson Bounds 278f, Körner 39f). The system is valid, universal and certain, but is not a set of statements about Space. If however we choose to read it as suggesting such statements, they will often turn out to be correct, in fact: and their correctness is an interesting empirical discovery, on each occasion; not a theorem known for certain or reliable in advance (cp Mackie 1966). The resulting 'geometry' concerns entities and relations invented and defined, i.e. contributed at choice, by us.

Kant's system played its part in the development of this more complex theory. Standing on his shoulders, we should not berate him for not seeing what we see. In particular, we should not suggest that our theory fulfils his criteria, for the 'certain' science is not a 'real' one, and the real, factual part is uncertain. It would be nearer the historical truth to say that the philosophical community has worked out this theory as a remarkable second-best, because any theory which did fulfil all his criteria would have consequences which are unacceptable.

*   *   *   *

Most people reject Transcendental Idealism (one such consequence) because, after all, tables and sideboards are obviously external, independent things, not just things-seen-or-heard ... , perceptibles, 'phenomena'. To turn the tables on this argument, or prejudice, Kant offers to show that Transcendental Realism if taken realistically would make Things even more dubious than his own theory was alleged to do. For if Space and Time were objectively real, two independent infinite insubstantial non-Things would have to be there first, before there could be any Thing at all - to avoid which paradox we would have to follow good old Berkeley and make things quite illusory! (B 56,70) Then again, if things perceived were really real, they would have to be inferred, unreliably, from our perceptions of them, leaving it still possible that maybe there are no such real external things ('empirical idealism'); whereas if it is things-as-perceived that we see and feel and hear, we do perceive them directly and need not worry about the

V.24 Refuting certain sets of views

possible slips twixt cup and lip which inference will always bring (A 369f).

These two refutation-sketches do not disprove Transcendental Realism, but they may make that doctrine unattractive to persons holding certain other views. They do not, however, bring in the argument from science.

Note C. The Sciences of Time. We put our perceptions in temporal order. This makes it possible for us to have a science of Time. Which science is that supposed to be? Some say arithmetic (Walker 71; Wilkerson 35). Kant says
   Pure mathematics considers space in geometry and time in pure mechanics. To these is to be added a certain concept, intellectual to be sure in itself but whose becoming actual in the concrete requires the auxiliary notions of time and space in the successive addition and simultaneous juxtaposition of separate units, which is the concept of number treated in arithmetic (Dissertation #12).
In the Critique, number is still treated as conceptual (A 103/B 104), yet achieved by intuitive construction with fingers, beads etc. (B 299). Abstract symbols provide the same constructive, insight-giving service to algebra (B 745, 762). In none of these passages is arithmetic or algebra presented as the science of Time.
   Kant's task is to show that physical science could be known by us. Dividing this up, he presents 1. timeless geometry as about Space alone; 2. pure mechanics (motion-alone, disregarding weight) as involving Space and Time; 3. pure physics (the rest of motion-science) as also involving Substance, Cause etc., noting that "pure mechanics can only form its concepts of motion with the aid of the representation of Time"(P #10, cp Broad 54).
   Every genuine science, on Kant's theory, must refer to items contributed by us. Algebra and Arithmetic do look like sciences. They will have to go in somewhere. When writing the Critique, Kant was still deciding where.

Chapter Six

OUR WORLD

Kant offered to explain our knowledge of worldly connections as derived from structural elements contributed by us to our experience. To show that Space is of this a priori character, he appeals to our possession of geometry, a sound deductive science. But this soundness would itself be in question, were we still enquiring just how Space comes into it. The argument back from the fact of science is thus p-circular. This weakness does not however affect the corresponding refutations: thus anyone granting a science of geometry, of a sort obtainable only on 'inside information', can properly be inhibited from saying Space is Real.

Kant's theory of physics is modelled on his theory of geometry. Does it also rely on an ineffective, backward argument?

25. RESPECTABLE ADDITIONS TO EXPERIENCE

The problem of scientific knowledge is solved if it relates to structural elements contributed by us: "for the mind can fully understand its own productions and designs" (B xiii).

Kant proposed this solution, for pure mathematics, in his inaugural Dissertation as professor (1770). He then extended it to 'mixed mathematics', in the Critique (1781). For this purpose he needs to show that the relevant concepts do originate with us: and to suggest how, by contributing them, we could arrive at the basic propositions of physics and geometry.

VI.25 Respectable additions to experience

At first sight his problem here, and his solution, run parallel to those for geometry. In detail, the argument diverges somewhat. For one thing, the debating position is rather different

All will agree that geometry is a proper science, and all need persuading that Space is contributed by us. Here Kant's main argument has to run back from the accepted fact of geometry to the disputed source and status of its subject-matter, Space. The theory of Transcendentalism is indeed paradoxical, but it is not dispensable. Indeed it is the Q E D of this whole section of the work.

In the case of physics, some doubted if it was a science, having learnt from Hume that Substance and Causation may be fictional. Kant needs to turn this argument around, but he need not, in doing so, persuade his readers that these concepts are contributed, for they think so already. So we hear rather less of the argument from science.

Given that some scientific concepts are contributed, and supposing some science could be founded on that fact, we must still decide which contributed-concepts are thus foundational. In Hume's critique any concept not deriving from experience is set aside as fictional: Cause, Thing, Person ... Kant first rescued Space and Time, leaving behind Substance, Cause and Force and all the 'bogus axioms' they generate (<u>Dissertation</u> #27f). In the Critique he plans to rescue more of them; but not all. He needs a little list, and for that list he needs a principle.

The idea of Cause serves always as a link: 'the-sun-shining-on-the-stone' is linked with 'the-stone-becoming-hot' by the notion 'causes-to-be-hot', i.e. 'heats'. So perhaps all the contributed-concepts, or categories, are linkage-concepts of various sorts. Now it seems that every statement we make and every thought we positively think does involve two elements linked together by an 'is'. Logicians have however distinguished several varieties of 'is':

    is equal to
    is of such and such a quality
    is in conseqence
    is and has to be ...

VI.25 Respectable additions to experience

Borrowing their list, let us match a category to each. All other would-be categories can then be thrown away as fictional.

Kant thought his little list could thus be settled once for all: the modes of human contribution-to-experience must be aspects of human nature itself, and so not open to diminution or development. Very few have been happy with the 'Transcendental Guiding-thread' he proposed for working out the final list; not that other suggestions on the matter have been any more acceptable.

Having finished his list, Kant still feels obliged to distinguish the items on it from the items off it, in some way. For the concepts listed <u>might</u> be bogus and surreptitious, list and all. We <u>need</u> some chain of authorities to vindicate our claim to them. This 'deduction' can hardly start from given experiences, so it will have to work 'transcendentally', by showing that just these are the concepts that make experience possible (B 117f).

If 'Cause' needs vindicating in this way, why not also 'Space' and 'Time'? Because spatial and temporal elements are incorporated in our perceptions automatically: as we perceive, they are just-given, 'intuited'. Causal linkage, however, is dispensable: we could say merely "the sun shone AND the stone got hot". So argument is needed to show that causal concepts and such-like do properly 'apply' to objects in our world. This is the real Q E D of this second section of the work.

All the same, Space and Time have already been transcendentally 'deduced' (B 119), apparently by showing that phenomenal objects are bound to be spatial and temporal, since the spatial and temporal aspects are inserted by us, in perceiving them. The Deduction of the Categories follows a similar basic strategy.

The 'Deduction' is to vindicate the advance-concepts on Kant's little list: not by showing where we got them from, but by proving our use of them to be 'all right'. For example, is it all right to apply to things the concept of physical influence ? - a question which Leibniz and Berkeley both answered in the negative (cp Mackie 91f).

VI.25 Respectable additions to experience

To see what this question involves, let us look at a parallel case. Astrologers employ in their work a concept of stellar influence, which links our good and bad fortune to what the planets are doing at the time. This concept may well be consistent. It has been worked up to an art, and set forth as a system, in several civilizations independently. Perhaps we could now reduce it to a science, with professors, research grants, learned journals and honorary doctorates. And one could still ask: Is there anything in it, after all?

That question can be asked about physics. We may grant the basic concepts, admire the scientific superstructure, even employ some of its results in daily life, and still ask: Is it guaranteed to work? We can apply those concepts, of course. Any set of concepts can be applied, to some extent, if we try hard enough. But do they match all the way along? Can we be sure <u>in the shop</u> that they will plug in to our experience?

26. PHYSICS IS O.K.

The strategy is to define the field of objects to which these advance-concepts will certainly apply, and then to claim that these are the only advance-concepts we can have herebelow, and are quite good enough for us.

Space and Time must come into all items-observed, as observing consists partly of our 'placing' items in a grid for temporal and spatial reference. The resulting observations make up our only world, so Space and Time although contributed must be true of it (B 59f). What more could one reasonably ask?

Substance, Cause, Quantity etc. need not come into our perceptions taken one by one, but the only way we know to put these together and make sense is to construct a scenario of durable, sizeable Things of several types, each with its regular Qualities and Powers. So these categories must come into all such Things, since Things come about only by our assembling them, using categories, from phenomena. This scientific world of Things is the only world we understand. So the categories by which we create it must be properly applied (A 129, P #21, B 163).

VI.26 Physics is O.K.

> Nature has much to teach us which we can't work out for ourselves, yet our enquiry into those mysteries must conform to what Nature gets from us. It was this insight that put physics on the high-road of a Science (B xiv).

What further vindication of the advance-concepts could anyone require?

That some advance-concepts or other will come in handy for speculating on the Universe, can hardly be denied. Even astrologers will agree to that. But Kant has to vindicate just the items on his little list. If he says 'just the concepts of pure physics' he will effectively rely on the argument from science, and the overall result will once again be p-circular. Instead, he extends the Deduction by an extra, early stage (cp Henrich 1969).

The extra and initial stage of the vindicating-argument is to show that in assembling Things we must use just those templates or modes-of-assembly to which the linking 'is' was said to correspond (Horstmann 1981). By these structural concepts the mind

> compares ideas, linking them or keeping them apart, thus transforming the raw material of sensible impressions into the finished product, that knowledge of objects which we call 'experience'(B 1).

Kant found this argument difficult to put, and we need not follow all its windings here. The main idea is that Things need assembling from sequences of distinct atomized phenomena; and that an Assembler is needed, to be doing this. He goes along and around fitting bits into the picture here and there, but these bits must first of all fit *him* - rather as a jig-saw can be done only with pieces that 'belong'. Now a jig-saw piece belongs if its bumps and dips are of the sort which other pieces of that picture also show, for interlocking with; but for Kant the modes-of-assembly are part of the Assembler's character. His repertoire of ways-of-unifying-bits thus selects the bits for him to unify: like a Macbeth Dramatic Club, open only to persons ready to enact and re-enact just those transactions and relationships which that play provides.

VI.26 Physics is O.K.

This selection ensures that the bits of sensory information we put together into Things and Processes can be put together in such ways. But do those Things and Processes make up a real world? Well, the world they make up is the only one that we shall ever know, so perhaps we should make do with it.

Categories are concepts which write the rule-book for phenomena and for the Nature which they constitute (B 163).

But why should Nature obey? Why should natural objects conform to our combination-laws? Why should the connections between Things and Processes exemplify just those types of linkage which knit together all my bits of sensory news as 'mine'?

All assembly is by the category-modes. Now even perception involves assembly. 'Experience' means knowing by linking perceptions up, which can be done only by the categories, so they hold good, in advance, for all objects of experience (B 161).

This line of reasoning recalls the argument to geometry: that Space being our contribution, the spatial relations of objects could be fully known by us. If the types of inside information which we are bound to contribute, by assembling Things, are of just the type pure physics does require, then the justification of physics is complete. Kant relied on his 'Transcendental Guiding-thread' to detect all the assembly-modes we use for Things, and hoped to show them sufficient by deriving from them all the acknowledged basic principles of science (Analytic of Principles, B 187 - 349).

This is Kant's contribution-theory for physics. It can now be compared with his contribution-theory for geometry, to bring out their divergences.

A contribution-theory involves three points, apparently independent and distinct:

A. that concepts X and Y are contributed by us
B. that our contributing concepts X and Y enables us to have science S,
C. that contributed-concepts X, Y do properly apply to or in some observational field.

VI.26 Physics is O.K.

Kant offers little argument for B, regarding it as evident.

A is presented (asserted) in the Metaphysical Exposition(B 38f) and the 'Metaphysical Deduction'(B 95f). For Space and Time, this is reinforced by the backward argument from the science of geometry. For the categories, such an argument is promised but not provided. Instead, the 'Guiding-thread' is used to pick out just those advance-concepts which are essential to science and Experience.

C is taken for granted, for geometry. Kant writes as though pennies were evidently circular, some fields and flags obviously triangular, and so on. His reason is that the forms of intuition are not optional: "the concepts of Space and Time, as items of knowledge-in-advance, are simply bound to apply to objects"(B 121). But does our having-to-see hexagons in honeycombs mean that this notion applies 'properly' to what the bees have made?

For the categories, C is considered at great length, with much ingenuity but only moderate success. As simple conditions of perceiving anything, categories would be as essential and unavoidable as the forms of Space and Time; but "they are not conditions for our observing things" (B 122). So a longer argument is attempted, to show that categories serve in putting observations together to make systematic sense.

In sum: B is taken for granted,
         A is argued, for geometry only,
         C is argued, for physics only.

This curious divergence can be partly explained by the debating position at the time. People needed persuading (A) that Space and Time were ideal, but not (C) that they applied. People did not need persuading that causal connections were unobservable (A); and in consequence they were inclined to doubt (C) if such conections appied to real things at all.

It may also be suggested that discussion of C, for physics, has in a curious way replaced discussion of A. If concepts X and Y obviously apply to and indeed constitute a certain range of objects R, we shall consider them as part of that experience, and shall not need persuading that they were indeed contributed by us. If on the other hand concepts X and Y are clearly imposed by us upon experience, our concern will be whether they 'fit' and 'belong' or are forced upon phenomena.

27. THE BEST PHYSICS WE HAVE

It may be urged that the construction-methods now in use for Things have made possible a science of Nature, of some sort: and that while it is no doubt good to be critical it is not wise to start by throwing away the only science we have. Abstract critiques and abstract justifications are about equally irrelevant. What matters is, it works.

It could further be said, in support, that it is unclear what sort of vindication Kant is looking for. He says we need to make good our claim to observational use of 'Substance', 'Cause', etc. He says that empirical concepts like 'dog' can be vindicated by producing one; but as advance-concepts are non-empirical, their justification must operate 'transcendentally', from the fact that knowledge does occur (B 119). In the complex argument that follows, however, we sometimes lose sight of this quite modest goal.

If Smith asks Brown whether 'subtracting' is really meaningful, a genuine idea with proper application to the real world, Brown would show him some take-away sums, and describe some occasions when he might want to 'take-away'. He can't do more. He can't produce 'subtraction' in some more concrete way, like producing a Yeti or a coelocanth to show the species is extant. He can only show the concept at work in some undoubted instances. For concepts even more basic this showing of instances may be less suggestive, more debatable: "Here, George, this gent does not believe in Cause or Substance or Degree, just show him one of each and send him off!"

Subtraction is something we do. Have we a 'right' to subtract? Well, we will if we like; and we shall like if we find the results make doing it worthwhile. 'Vindication' here means showing how it works and that it pays. Now Kant claims to have shown that it is the basic concepts of physics that we use in making any sense at all of our experience. Anyone who grants that claim but is dissatisfied with the results had better just stop doing it.

VI.27 The best physics we have

On this view the 'question of justification', correctly understood, can be answered simply by showing how the concept in question 'works'. The answer may need to be filled out, as physics develops, but Kant's version will do for a start (cp Rorty 1977, Körner *Transcendental* 1966).

But Kant was tackling a critical problem: how is natural science possible?(P #5 = B 20). What right have we to take it for granted that it does work (that the results of physics are reliable) while still explaining how it works, in order to show that such a science is possible?

28. WE KNOW THAT PHYSICS IS ALL RIGHT

If we don't trust Kant's Guiding-thread, and find his derivations of physical principles a little dubious, we can take his Deduction only as suggesting 'synthetically' how we do in fact assemble Things. We can then say that these methods seem to work, and have been quite good enough for members of our family - and look at me now! If this dogmatic complacency proves unacceptable, we may be driven to say that categories are needed for the Things and properties which physics is about, therefore it must be quite alright to use them every day. And this would be an argument from the fact of science, 'analytic' and p-circular. Anyone using this argument in proof may be asked which he has in mind to prove, the conclusion or the premises.

Such an argument could of course serve in refutation of a certain set of views: for anyone holding that categories are needed, etc, and that physics is a real science had better not deny that such categories can be properly applied to whatever items physics is about. If you want physics, categories are something you cannot afford to be without.

There is not much difference between asking: You want Physics, don't you? and saying: You have got physics, haven't you? So the refutation, which is all the argument from science can actually provide, turns out very like the view that only practical justifications are practical.

29. DOES KANT ARGUE BACK FROM PHYSICS?

Does Kant's theory of physics involve the analytic, p-circular argument from science?

As first presented, no. The theory has three steps. First, a suggested way to finalize a list of our contributions to the sciences ('Metaphysical Deduction' B 95 - 116); next, a long and tortuous account of how we come to make those contributions, while making sense of life and things (Transcendental Deduction Stage I); finally, a claim that our contributions are, by that very fact, completely knowable by us (T.D.Stage II)

Prolegomena offers to answer 'analytically' the question "How is natural science possible?" but in fact re-hashes the 'synthetic' Deduction from the Critique. The revised version of this given in the second edition does distinguish between Stages I and II, but does not fulfil the promise of 'analytic' argument which the new Introduction repeats from Prolegomena.

Kant's theory is:

> Pure physics (as a deductive system of universal but non-analytic laws knowable in advance of the relevant experience) can be known true of Things if and only if the structural elements (for assembling perceptions with) are contributed by us.

The Deduction spells out the if-bit, showing how our contributions would make physics possible. The only-if bit is taken pretty much for granted: observation alone cannot provide deductive science.

The theory is not used to show that Substance, Cause etc. are contributed: that was already accepted (with regret). Instead, some labour goes into closing the list of contributed-concepts, and much into showing that those concepts do apply: i.e. that the science built with them will be a science of the real world. It is at this stage, we suggest, that Kant's argument is most in need of support: from Pragmatism, or from a p-circular argument from the fact of science.

There is a third view, on which the Deduction has little to do with physics and

VI.29 Does Kant argue back from physics?

everything to do with Things. Things need assembling, assembling requires an Assembler, some perceptive and reflective unifying agent over and above the observations unified (a 'Transcendental Unity of Apperception'), and this Assembler can only work in his native unifying-modes, which must therefore turn up in all the resulting Things and Processes (cp Meyer 1981, Ameriks 1982).

This version seems closer to the text but further from Kant's ultimate purposes. It establishes an 'I', an advance-concept if ever one was, and doubted only by Hume (though missing from Kant's little lists). It leaves physics over to be vindicated in the Analytic of Principles. It makes the justification of the Categories so exactly parallel to the argument for phenomena (B 52f) that it could hardly have taken Kant ten years to evolve and thirty-five close and difficult pages to explain.

On this view the Deduction, whether successful or not, is entirely synthetic, with no danger of p-circularity; and the real work is left to a later argument, for which that danger will recur.

30. COGITO ERGO SUNT RES

Kant has many other transcendental arguments. Each starts from some given item of knowledge, and concludes to some 'prior' fact which 'makes that knowledge possible'. Those already considered set out from a public system of guaranteed knowledge, a Science. In the 'Refutation of Idealism' the argument starts out from something each reader realizes for himself: that he is thinking now. This private recognition is said to require the existence of public, continuing external Things (cp Aquila 1979).

This argument is meant to <u>prove</u> that external things exist. It would thus refute both sorts of Idealism: dogmatic (we know they don't exist independently), and problematic (we can't be sure they do).

According to Kant, I don't just realize that I exist, but that I am-existing-at-such-and-such-a-time. This timing, he says, requires permanent external Things, against which to reckon the flux of

VI.30 Cogito ergo sunt res

time in my sequence of ideas. So I could not realize, as I do, that "it's now I am", unless there were such Things about, to use as clocks.

This argument employs extra and clearly contingent premisses, such as "all timing requires permanent external things, as clocks". Its overall shape is however similar to those already analysed:

1. The statement "I am (now)" requires permanent external things, as clocks.
2. "I am (now)" is undeniable.
So 3. There are external things.

Here 2 could not be known before 3, if 1 is true, so there is built-in circularity. The argument is incompetent as proof of 3, though it is certainly valid and the premisses appear quite plausible.

Will the argument serve in refutation? That is, can it rightly be used to dissuade someone who holds 2 from denying 3? Yes, presumptive circularity is no obstacle to such a use. The inconsistency of holding 1 and 2 but denying 3 remains, even if progress from 1 and 2 to 3 is impermissible. So if Smith, the well-known problematical idealist, goes around saying that Smith is, but things are dubious, anyone who agrees with premiss 1 can tell him that things like clocks are as certain as anyone's "I am", since 'I-am'-ing itself requires clocks.

Premiss 1 may be less evident to us than it seemed to Kant. Timing, he says, "always requires some continuant perceived, which can't be in me, for it is by this continuant that I am being timed" (B 275). This recalls the argument that the concepts of Time and Space cannot be gleaned from experience, since they would be needed first, for us to have those distinct experiences (B 38, 46). This argument works, if 'first' means 'first in time'; but requirement or presupposition involves logical, not temporal, priority.

Premiss 1 would be refuted if anyone managed to time his experiences without using any external things, as clocks, just by some recurring item in his sequence of ideas. There are obvious difficulties in our getting and presenting evidence of such a case, our culture being somewhat clock-bound. But we might be able to imagine such a Mind

VI.30 Cogito ergo sunt res

whose internal ticker timed everything for him. If his fictional goings-on can be consistently described then there is no necessity in Premiss 1. And if there is no necessity in the matter, it is far from clear what could serve as evidence (Palmer 1972; cp Stevenson 1982).

31. KANT'S REMAINING THEORIES

The arguments so far considered all fit together in a step-ladder:
   a. Our knowledge of geometry requires that perception be phenomenal;
   b. Our knowledge of physics requires a continuing 'I', using categories, to assemble perceived phenomena into Things and Processes;
   c. A continuing and self-conscious 'I' requires distinct continuing other Things as well.

All these arguments suffer from presumptive circularity, so can provide no proof. Yet all supply compelling reasons to grant the conclusion IF one insists on sticking by the premisses: they do work ad hominem.

How does this leave Kant's theory of knowledge? How much of his system can stand, if all his 'transcendental' proofs are undermined?

If the points which he argues transcendentally were also proved by some other argument, our critique would only remove an unnecessary extra strut. But Kant has no other sufficient arguments to prove these points. As he emphasized repeatedly, he had been able to go beyond his predecessors only because he discovered and exploited this new type of argument (A xii, B xvi, 24, 748).

*   *   *   *

The precise interpretation of Kant's great theory has been and will remain a matter of dispute. It does look as though he meant to argue back from geometry and physics as given sciences; yet it also seems plausible to suggest that his reasoning took some other route (cp Guyer 1982). That he always followed the same route, can be denied with

VI.31 Kant's remaining theories

considerable confidence. That he always knew just how he was arguing, seems open to reasonable doubt.

Our claim is: that the interpretation just given fits in with very many things he says; that it yields a clear and persuasive line of reasoning which Kant could well regard as new; that this line of reasoning is ineffective, for the reasons we have given, which Kant could well have failed to appreciate.

Just suppose we are wrong in attributing this line of thought to Kant. The position then is this: it just happens that Kant's texts of the 1780's lend themselves to a misinterpretation invented two centuries later, which just happens to illustrate a line of reasoning under vigorous discussion at that later time, which in spite of its name had nothing at all to do with Kant. In this case we can be grateful that what Kant did not mean to say does happen to show up clearly an insidious defect in this modern line of reasoning.

Readers disinclined for historical dispute can thus benefit from our 'Kantian' example without first deciding just how far it is due to Kant.

Chapter Seven

HOW PRESUPPOSITION WORKS

The argument in Descartes' <u>Cogito</u> relies on 'presupposition', and moves 'back' from some presupposing item to the constituent it presupposed. This move involves a sort of circularity, the presupposed constituent being needed at the outset, to ensure the propriety of the item presupposing it.

The central arguments of Kant's <u>Critique</u> also turn on presupposition, and involve circularity. But the presuppositions in Kant's arguments are not quite the same as those relied on by Descartes. The <u>Cogito</u> works by referential presupposition, by the fact that every 'think' requires an 'I'. But Kant is considering how we can come to think of A as a 'substance' which is having a certain 'quality', B, or of C as the 'cause' of D. The presuppositions he investigates are thus conceptual in character.

These two sorts of presupposition deserve further study. In particular, a comparison of their logical properties should show why they bear the same name, and how far inferences which turn on them should be relied upon. This enquiry may also reveal why presumptive circularity is so regularly found infecting backward arguments.

32. LOGICAL PROPERTIES OF PRESUPPOSITION

Referential presupposition is a logical relation between a statement S, and P, one of its constituents, whereby the untruth of P makes S improper. So 'S presupposes P' indicates that the truth of P is a necessary condition for the propriety of S. To express these points, let us use quotation-marks to symbolize propriety:

84

VII.32 Logical properties of presupposition

                                          ("S"   means   S is proper)
             'S presupposes P'   means   "S" only if P
So 'S presupposes P'   entails   "S" entails P

On this account, IF S presupposes P THEN S is improper whenever P is untrue (false or inappropriate). But the converse does not hold. For S to presuppose P, it is not enough that S be improper on all the right occasions, i.e. WHENEVER P is untrue. S must be improper for the right reason, viz. BECAUSE P is untrue.

(1) <u>Presupposition is transitive.</u> Given that S presupposes P, and P presupposes Q, does it follow that S presupposes Q? In our symbolism, this is less than obvious

$$("S" \rightarrow P) \cdot ("P" \rightarrow Q) \quad \overset{?}{\quad} \quad ("S" \rightarrow Q$$

for the second P has quotation marks while the first one is without. However, if we grant that truth requires propriety, P $\rightarrow$ "P", this can be inserted on the left to complete the formal inference. That is: IF Q is false THEN P is inappropriate AND SO untrue, THEREFORE S is inappropriate.

2. <u>Presupposition works both ways.</u> If Johnny did not sit for his exam then he did not do well in it, nor badly either. Both results equally would presuppose that he did sit. Presupposition always 'works both ways', so that from either presupposition the other can also be inferred; thus from "His doing badly in the exam presupposes that he sat for it" IT FOLLOWS THAT "His doing well in the exam presupposes that he sat for it", and conversely:

$$(\text{"S"} \rightarrow P) \qquad (\text{"not-S"} \rightarrow P)$$

This unusual feature, whereby 'sauce for the goose is sauce for the gander too', has so far no official name. Let us mark it by calling presupposition 'ganderous'.

3. <u>Presupposition involves three values.</u> It could be argued that as Johnny must have either done well or not done well, he simply must have sat for the exam; for truth and falsity are exhaustive alternatives, and (we are now told) both require propriety. In the same way: George's peas either

VII.32 Logical properties of presupposition

are in bloom or are not in bloom, so he must have a garden either way - a brisk method for establishing general horticultural truths about the universe! These arguments work by covert appeal to a principle which no longer holds. Bivalence ('it is or it isn't') can be relied on in many contexts, but not where impropriety can occur. Presupposition is essentially three-valued: true, false, or inappropriate (Haack 66f).

4. **Presupposition is irreflexive.** Can a statement presuppose itself? If so, it would not only be proper when true, but also true whenever proper: EITHER true (and proper) OR improper, but never false.

Statements with these properties can be constructed easily:

S Mrs Phillips at no. 64 is a married woman.
T No carnivores are vegetarians.

These statements however presuppose only 'Mrs Phillips', 'carnivores', and perhaps 'No. 64': they do not presuppose the statements S and T. Not even as a limiting case could we say that the truth of those statements (or any others) makes possible their propriety, by providing referees. The 'pre-' in 'presupposition' cannot be overlooked. So presupposition is an irreflexive relationship, like 'taller' and unlike 'identical'.

5. **Presupposition is anti-symmetrical.** If two statements S and T presupposed each other, the propriety of S would require the truth of T, and therefore its propriety, which in turn would require the truth of S. So S would presuppose itself. And so would T. But that has just been shown to be impossible. And clearly if T is needed 'first' to provide a refereee for S, it can't rely on S for a similar provision, not without circularity. So presupposition is an anti-symmetrical relationship, like 'father', and unlike 'relative'.

6. **Presupposition is directional.** In some sense the item presupposed has to be there 'first' (hence the 'pre-'). But not first in time; P need not be true in the morning so that S can be proper in the afternoon. The priority we intend is logical in character; that P is needed for S or for any of its alternatives, as eggs and other things are needed

VII.32 Logical properties of presupposition

for making any sort of omelette. Thus the truth of P is a necessary <u>but not sufficient</u> condition for the propriety of S; much as Bertie's Aunt Jemima's being a female is a necessary but not sufficient condition for her being Bertie's aunt.

There is a slight confusion here over names. We do distinguish a necessary-and-sufficient condition (parent's parent = grandparent) from one which is only described as necessary (mother's brother only if uncle). But we allow this 'only-if' to be applied in cases which are really 'if-and-only-if' (perhaps because the sufficiency is not yet clear to us). Thus one could say that a necessary condition of labelling a drink 'sherry' is that it be a fortified white wine grown around Jerez, when in fact the name can be applied to anything fulfilling all those conditions, as those are all the conditions that there are. But this easy-going usage means that we have no common term for a condition which is definitely not sufficient, though it be a necessary one, as being-a-female is definitely necessary but quite definitely not sufficient to being-an-aunt. Let us set aside the word 'requires' for this use:

B is a nec + suff c for A = A equivalent to B
B is a nec + maybe suff c for A = A implies B
B is a nec + <u>not</u> suff c for A = A requires B

We can use a tailed arrow ⤳ for 'requires'.

Referential presupposition, then, is
1. transitive,
2. ganderous (if S presupposes P so does not-S)
3. non-bivalent (three values are involved)
4. irreflexive,
5. anti-symmetrical,
6. directional (propriety of S requires truth of P).

These logical properties do not suffice to define the relation, but they do distinguish it from entailment, which is

1. transitive,
2. non-ganderous,
3. bivalent,
4. reflexive,
5. non-symmetrical,
6. non-directional.

VII.32 Logical properties of presupposition

Presupposition, the stronger relation, entails the weaker one; for if the truth of P is needed for the propriety of S, then it must be needed also for its truth, as truth requires propriety:

$$(\text{"S"} \rightarrow P) . (S \rightarrow \text{"S"}) \rightarrow (S \rightarrow P)$$

If S presupposes P, then a fortiori S entails P. So presupposition <u>is</u> not, but does <u>entail</u> entailment (cf Nerlich 1965, Ginsberg 1972).

Presupposition is more obvious in some constructions, which are favoured in certain languages. Thus in Greek or Tamil we might meet a nesting structure of participles

((having come) and having seen) I conquered

which relates the facts quite explicitly; whereas Caesar's Latin formula just narrated three separate events and left the hearer to put in their relationship. Hebrew also is said to be 'paratactic' in this way, i.e. to recite events merely conjoined and leave the audience to work out how they really stand. This may leave the curious or finicky wondering: Did the Second Commandment contain two prohibitions, a. not to make graven images, and b. not to worship them, or did it just rule out image-making-for-worship-purposes ?

33. LIMITATIONS ON INFERENCE

Given two statements, a, b, and told whether they are true or not, we can work out whether the complex statement 'a and b' is true. No knowledge of context or even of meaning is required: truth-values are enough. So the connective 'and' is said to be 'truth-functional'.

Some logical relations are plainly not truth-functional. You cannot tell from truth-values alone whether b follows from a. You may discover that b is true whenever a is so, but 'whenever' is not good enough, you need 'because'. So context and meaning must come into it. The same goes for the converse relationship, 'implies'. But we can construct a truth-functional connective which behaves rather like 'implies'; and this manufactured analogue, 'materially implies' has in fact proved very useful in the symbolic calculus.

VII.33 Limitations on inference

Presupposition is clearly not <u>truth-</u> functional, as three values are involved. Nor is it even 'functional', i.e. the values alone of S and P do not suffice to determine whether S presupposes P. Only inspection of S and detection of P as its ingredient can establish this relationship. Consideration of content and meaning is required. The relation has to be seen, to be believed. It cannot be inferred. Take for example

S All John's children are in bed

and suppose (i) John has children, (ii) he hasn't. In case (i), S is proper; in case (ii), improper. But this can only be made out by seeing what S presupposes and checking whether it is true. Propriety and impropriety cannot be seen, but have to be inferred.

The position then is this:

1. We cannot make out whether S presupposes P just from the values (truth, propriety ..) of S and P,
2. We can make out that S is proper only by inference from P's truth and S's presupposing P,
3. The 'values of S and P' are therefore not available until we know whether S presupposes P.

Propriety is thus 'internal' to the presupposing relationship, i.e. not accessible independently. This is bound to restrict the scope for inference from presupposition.

As presupposition involves a necessary condition, inferences from presupposition run parallel to the four moods of hypothetic inference. Thus given that S presupposes P we may reason

1. but S is proper, therefore P is true   (AA)
2. but P is untrue, therefore S is improper   (DC)
3. but P is true , therefore S is proper   (AC)
4. but S is improper, therefore P is untrue   (DA)

Moods AC and DA are plainly invalid. A sufficient condition would be needed, to enforce such conclusions: e.g. 'S presupposes <u>only</u> P'.

Mood DC is valid, and is our only means for detecting impropriety: we see that S presupposes P, note that P is untrue, and infer impropriety in S. This mood is in regular and profitable use.

89

VII.33 Limitations on inference

Mood AA is equally valid, but unusable. Given the truth of P as a necessary condition for the propriety of S, we can rely on the propriety of S as sufficient condition for the truth of P. But 'the propriety of S' is not available, except by seeing what S presupposes and verifying that presupposition as correct. Propriety is an internal feature, so reasoning back from it is bound to be p-circular. Mood AA is therefore incompetent as proof.

*   *   *   *

It may be helpful, at this point, to consider a value-table appropriate to this relationship, and examine its properties (though readers who decide to skip to #34 will not miss anything essential to the later argument).

A value-table will present the values taken by 'S presupposes P' for each of the nine possible value-combinations of its constituents, S and P.

Having nine places, the value-table is best presented solid, as an array. The values of S appear on the left, those of P at the top. The resulting values for 'S presupposes P' occupy the nine places inside the array.

		(P)		
		T	F	I
	T	1	2	3
(S)	F	4	5	6
	I	7	8	9

(i) If S presupposes P then S is improper whenever P is untrue; so S cannot presuppose P where proper values of S combine with untrue P. So we enter F in places 2,3,5,6.

	T	F	I
T	1	F	F
F	4	F	F
I	7	8	9

(ii) If S presupposes P then P must be true whenever S is proper, so S can presuppose P when S is proper and P true. Can, not must. So while S's presupposing P does sanction certain value-combinations of S and P as appropriate, the occurrence of those combinations of values does not show definitely that S presupposes P.

	T	F	I
T	?	F	F
F	?	F	F
I	?	?	?

VII.33 Limitations on inference

We can in fact find many instances of S and P for which S does not presuppose P even though these values are fulfilled. Thus the statement "It's Tuesday today" is usually proper, yet does not presuppose "3 x 2 = 6", although this latter statement is true.

Let us go back to first principles. According to our definition, 'S presupposes P' means

truth of P required for propriety of S

So where S presupposes P we can't have

S proper and at the same time P untrue

Using this condition we can devise a new but analogous relationship, called POSES:

S poses P = NOT - (S is proper and P untrue)

We shall declare that whenever this condition is met then S poses P. That is, we license ourselves to move not only from 'poses' to certain value-combinations but also back again.

We now try to complete the table, for this new relationship.

(i) Where proper values of S do combine with untrue P, it is false that S poses P. So we enter F in places 2,3,5,6.

	T	F	I
T	1	F	F
F	4	F	F
I	7	8	9

(ii) Where S takes improper values or P is true or both, there S poses P. So we enter T in places 1,4,7,8,9.

	T	F	I
T	T	F	F
F	T	F	F
I	T	T	T

Note that the Fs for POSES correspond exactly to those for PRESUPPOSE, but that POSES has Ts where PRESUPPOSE has question-marks (meaning that <u>maybe</u> S presupposes P). So, given that S does presuppose P (which must be in a place marked ?, as all the rest show F), then surely S poses P. So S presupposing P implies S posing P.

VII.33 Limitations on inference

Given that S poses P, the propriety of S (its being either true or false) requires the truth of P (as places 2,3,5,6 show an F); and of course the truth of S would require its propriety (S can't be both true and improper); so the truth of S requires the truth of P. That is, POSES implies IMPLIES.

Some other logical properties of POSES resemble those of PRESUPPOSE:

1. <u>Posing is transitive.</u> If P poses Q, the untruth of Q will make P improper, thus causing impropriety in S, if S poses P; and if the untruth of Q makes S improper then S poses Q (places 8,9).
2. <u>Posing is ganderous.</u> For the first two lines in the table are identical, and can be swopped.
3. <u>Posing is three-valued.</u> T,F,I.

In other respects, POSES and PRESUPPOSE are quite different:

4. <u>Posing is non-reflexive.</u> A statement can pose itself; e.g. one which is never false but always either true or inappropriate. So any tautology will pose itself, as will any statements presupposing a necessary falsity ("the speed of virtue is 37 mph"). And there may be statements whose internal structure permits now truth, now impropriety, but never falsity. So posing is non-reflexive: for some S, S poses S.
5. <u>Posing is non-symmetrical.</u> Any pair of permanent truths will pose each other. So will any couple of perpetual improprieties. Posing can be mutual.

Like presupposing, posing is transitive and ganderous and implies 'implies'. Unlike presupposing, posing is non-reflexive and non-symmetrical. These differences derive from posing being functional in character.

Given that S poses P, S can be proper only if P be true. This necessary condition can be used in argument, in the same four familiar moods:

1. but S is proper so P must be true   (AA)
2. but P is untrue so S is improper   (DC)
3. but P is true so S must be proper   (AC)
4. but S is improper so P cannot be true (DA)

VII.33 Limitations on inference

Moods AC and DA are plainly invalid. Mood DC is valid, and useful for eliciting impropriety. Mood AA is valid but unusable, as the propriety of S cannot be confirmed without first verifying P. For an improper statement <u>looks</u> just the same as its proper counterpart. Both mean, or would mean, the same: their difference lies in their relation to the facts. Propriety, then, cannot be detected merely by inspecting sentences. One must see what matters of fact are therein presupposed, and then see if those facts are really thus and so.

An argument back from S posing P to the truth of P turns out just as ineffective as an argument back from S presupposing P. Both are presumptively circular. This defect, then, is not due just to presupposition being a non-functional relationship, but to the way in which propriety and its absence become evident to us.

POSES, we said, is an 'analogue' to PRESUPPOSE. To see what this means in practice, it may be worth considering some possible 3-value analogues to our 2-valued connective 'materially implies': the 2-value table would appear top left, in places 1,2,4,5; place 3 needs an F, and the other four places are to be filled 'by policy', i.e. informed choice (cp Stiver 1975, Humberstone + 1976, Bergmann 1981).

There are 242 other analogues to PRESUPPOSE (5 places to fill, three choices for each). Some of the resulting calculi will be of considerable intrinsic interest - for those who like that sort of thing.

34. CONCEPTUAL INGREDIENCE

Lying presupposes truth-tellers.
Figure supposes extension.
Without property, there could be no damages.
You can only cross-examine witnesses.
You couldn't pretend to be a waiter if there were no real ones.
Individuals are prior to the classes that they constitute.
Suffering depends on craving which depends on wrongly thinking that you are a Self.
I can't have more pudding, I haven't yet had some.

93

VII.34 Conceptual ingredience

In each of these cases one item, A, is said to require another item, B; so that B could occur without A but not A on its own. A and B are concepts, and B is a constituent or essential part or basis of A: let us call it an 'ingredient'. It is often said in such cases that A presupposes B, but clearly not quite in the sense considered earlier. For the moment, let us call the relation one of 'conceptual ingredience'.

Ingredience is directional; i.e. B is a necessary part of A, but only a part, so A cannot also be a part of B, nor can A be ingredient in A. Ingredience is clearly transitive, for if C is needed for B and B for A then C is ingredient in A as well. Conceptual ingredients nest one in another, like a Chinese Box.

We use concepts not only in speaking and writing but also in looking and doing: for our concept of something will affect our treatment of it and even the way we see it and make sense of it. Some friends, out for a walk, may all notice the same thing hovering in the sky above the moors. One sees it as a bird, one as a hawk, a third (a bird-watcher) as a hawk-looking-for-prey, and a fourth (a shepherd) as a hawk-looking-for-prey-and-just-about-to-swoop. Clearly these more particular and detailed recognitions involve or presuppose those that are more general: not that one has to go through those before coming to these, for the trained recognition will be instantaneous; but just that one could not recognize it as a hawk and then deny it was a bird. But one might allow it was a bird but claim it was an eagle or a crow: it can't be a hawk and not a bird, but it might be some other sort of bird. This feature is distantly analogous to ganderosity: if presupposition P is needed for the truth of S then it is also needed for its falsity; and being-a-bird, which is needed for being-a-hawk, is also needed for being-an-eagle or a crow. Let us call this property 'indifference'.

Conceptual ingredience, like referential presupposition, is transitive, irreflexive, anti-symmetric, directional and non-functional. It is not ganderous, but it is indifferent. These resemblances in logical force sufficiently explain our use of 'presuppose' for both relationships (cp Rescher 1961).

VII.34 Conceptual ingredience

In ordinary converse we do not remark on conceptual ingredience, or trouble to define our terms, since we take their meanings and limits as pretty well agreed. But we may on occasion point out that B needs to be understood before tackling A. Thus if Smith has not mastered multiplication yet he will have no chance at all with square roots; and Jones will never appreciate a shaggy dog story until he notices that other stories always lead up to some 'point', dramatic or humorous.

"But one might learn 'hawk' first, from examples, and the generic 'bird-of-prey' long afterwards? Yes indeed, just as children get to say 'father' very early on, but 'male' and 'parent' fairly late, whereupon the true definition can dawn as a discovery. On the other hand, there can be few who learn 'rhombus' before grasping 'parallel'. So 'father' and 'hawk' only show that we may get to apply some words to the right individuals before grasping what they fully mean. Our consequent education in these matters may involve reference to presupposition or ingredience. And in dealing with well-defined terms from theories and systems, a grasp of their ingredients is usually pre-requisite.

35. SYSTEMS OF INGREDIENTS

It is no accident that our examples came from specialized sub-departments of speech like golf and arithmetic. In these areas technical terms have been worked out and formally defined; and it is here that conceptual ingredience can be determined with exactitude. 'Presupposition' is itself a term of art for describing the relations between definitions or concepts in a well-organized system. In such a system the order of introduction of the terms defined determines their inter-relation and so governs the structure of the system; rather as, in a deductive system, the choice of axioms and the order of their combination in proofs of the theorems determines the inter-relation between the theorems and so governs the structure of the system as a whole.

To see how words and their concepts can be ordered in a systematic way let us consider some technical handbook, e.g. on carpentry. The glossary will offer definitions of all the technical terms required in that speciality: definitions framed

VII.35 Systems of ingredients

mainly in non-technical language (which is assumed to need no explanation), but also employing some technical terms which are themselves defined elsewhere in the glossary. Suppose we underline these:

screwdriver-blade = blade of <u>screwdriver</u>

Now we sort out as 'basic' all those definitions in which no words are underlined, and allot one asterisk each to the terms which they define:

*screw = tapered and threaded metal nail

Next we collect definitions containing one-asterisk terms, underlined, and give two asterisks to the terms that they define

**screwdriver = tool for turning and so driving home a <u>screw</u>

And so on. The resulting little pyramids of definition will exhibit visually a complex linguistic structure, whose constituent relations can be described one by one in statements of presupposition or ingredience.

It sometimes happens that two or more terms need to be introduced together. Thus in explaining our society to a unisex visitor from Mars, we might need to expound the concept 'marriage', and along with it 'husband' and 'wife'. Neither of these has logical priority; a husband can be a husband only by being married to some wife, and a wife can be ... Such terms are collateral; both are essential to the institution of marriage, and both are introduced along with it. The same applies to other cases of so-called 'mutual presupposition', and to terms introduced in 'clusters': rule - agreement - same; proposition - true - false; function - argument; player - spectator - game.

It is sometimes said that A 'necessarily' presupposes B, but it is not clear what this means. The relation of presupposition does involve an element of necessity, but in all cases equally, so that hardly seems worth mentioning. Perhaps it means that B must be referred to, in defining A. This suggests that some other items in the definition of A are merely optional, or have alternatives, whereas B is unavoidable.

VII.35 Systems of ingredients

In a fully articulated system of concepts, such special necessity could have no place. The defined concepts are what they are in virtue of the definitions given: thus if A is defined as one species of the genus B then that definition constitutes A and makes B an ingredient in it. No ingredients are optional, once the system is worked out, so there is no point in calling any of them necessary.

For much of the time, however, we work with partly defined systems, trying to improve their structure by revising the definitions which link up the terms. Here one could sensibly enquire whether a certain item should or should not feature as ingredient in a certain term. Should 'democracy' be defined in terms of popular power, or range of alternative regimes, or electoral procedures? In such a case a claim that A <u>must</u> be defined in terms of B would at least make sense; though the claimant will still have to explain how he perceives this alleged necessity.

36. INFERENCES FROM INGREDIENCE

Conceptual presupposition has been stated as 'A requires B'. What is B a necessary condition of? Of the 'availability' of concept A, which cannot be deployed or put to use if its ingredient B is not available. This may be said of individuals: that Smith cannot appreciate a certain satire because he has not understood as pathos or bombast the styles being satirized, or that Brown could not possibly cheat on the shopping because he cannot add and has yet to grasp 'giving an account'. But the question whether concept B is available may also be raised in a well-defined system, such as symbolic logic or arithmetic, or in a carefully defined, specialized vocabulary such as that of the law. Here the question means: Has B been duly defined within the system? Had the definer of A a 'right' to this ingredient? - i.e. a right within the conventions of that linguistic institution which he proposes to reform? Kant's 'question of right'(B 116) is thus relative to the sciences that he has in mind. In our day the question 'Is it scientific?' has the same limitation and the same effect.

If A conceptually presupposes B, then B is an ingredient needed for defining A. On this necessary

VII.36 Inferences from ingredience

condition arguments both good and bad can be base As before, Denying the Antecedent (mood DA) is sure to be a fallacy, as is Affirming the Consequent (AC), for no <u>necessary</u> can support such inference. Argument in the other two moods occurs quite frequently. An example of Denying the Consequent, given earlier, seems sound and usable:

>   George has not mastered multiplication
>   So he cannot deal with square roots.   (DC)

Argument by Affirming the Antecedent also occurs:

>   They know what lying is (they lie)
>   So they must understand what it is to tell the
>   truth, seeing that is presupposed.   (AA)

This is valid, but unusable in proof. To argue:

>   A presupposes B
>   A is available
> So B is too

one needs some <u>other</u> way of telling that A is in order. But the only way is to see what its ingredients are and make sure they are all available - including B. As long as B is dubious on these grounds it cannot be made any less so by this sort of backward argument.

The statement that A presupposes B is always relative to some system of thought or of ideas. Ingredience is a feature of the system, not just of the ingredient concept and of that which presupposes it. We commonly neglect to mention the system, because it is so obvious. Definitions are constructional elements in systems of ideas, and ingredience results from defining A in terms of B. Thus when Locke says

>   the idea of liberty is the idea of a power in
>   any agent to do or forbear any particular
>   action, according to the determination or
>   thought of the mind, whereby either of them is
>   preferred to the other ... so that liberty
>   cannot be where there is no thought (II.21.#9)

we observe that <u>for Locke</u> and perhaps <u>for his age</u>, liberty presupposes thought. Restrictions of this sort should limit the general metaphysical conclusions drawn from statements of ingredience.

VII.36 Inferences from ingredience

It may happen that one well-defined system takes some of its basic terms from another. Physics is related to mathematics in this way: the definitions and procedures of mathematics are taken for granted at the start. It may then quite properly be said, that physics presupposes mathematics: meaning simply, that mathematical terms are ingredient in the basic terms of physics (cp Bubner 1977, Stebbing 176).

Mathematics is ingredient in physics because mathematics was created first and was then used in thinking out physical realities. But it can happen that such a relation is created afterwards, between two systems of thought already in existence. Thus a way may be found to define the basic notions of arithmetic in terms taken from logic and set theory, but <u>after</u> arithmetic has been worked out in systematic form. It is then said that arithmetic is 'reducible' to logic, meaning that its basic notions can be defined in logical terms, and that no extra notions, peculiar to arithmetic, are required (as physics did require some extra and peculiar notions, such as 'force'). So the statement 'T reduces to V' is stronger that 'T presupposes V', and equivalent to 'T presupposes only V'; i.e. no terms except those of V are required in defining the basic terms of T.

37. PRINCIPLES AND PREMISSES

The term 'presuppose' is also used to relate an incomplete argument to those missing premisses whose addition would make it satisfactory. Thus:

Smith   God must exist, for no earthly origin could account for this very grand idea which everybody has.
Brown   Your argument presupposes that every cause is at least as grand as its effect.

Here Brown remarks on an unstated assumption of Smith's, an extra premiss needed to complete his argument. This extra premiss is indeed 'required', but only for the goodness of Smith's argument. This relation is transitive, non-functional and directional, and hence irreflexive and symmetrical. That explains our using here again the term 'presuppose' (cp Stove 42, Balasubramanian 1979).

VII.37 Principles and premisses

Brown may reject Smith's argument A as inconclusive, complaining that the extra premiss P is not available, i.e. not proven, or not generally known, or not agreed by Brown. This complaint is precisely parallel to earlier Denials of the Consequent. It seems quite in order to argue

    A logically presupposes P
    P is not available
So A is inconclusive

Indeed shortfall of necessary premisses is one major way to establish inconclusiveness in arguments.

The other valid mood (AA) looks quite implausible:

    A logically presupposes P
    Argument A is conclusive
So P must be available, to argue from

For how could one tell that A is conclusive, except by checking that it has a valid form and that we have all the needful premisses? So one would have to establish P <u>before</u> starting on this argument.

Such an inference is clearly incompetent as proof. It might however be used against someone who asserts the conclusiveness of A while treating P as false or dubious. In this 'personal' use, to point out inconsistency, the inference can stand.

When we say Smith's argument requires P, do we mean the argument Smith stated or the one he meant to state? There is some danger of confusion here. The argument he stated, A, was invalid, and that invalid argument cannot be 'made valid' by adding extra premisses. It is what it is, an argument with insufficient premisses. Brown notes that there is another argument B, consisting of A + P, and that B is valid. Brown may charitably decide that B was the argument Smith 'really had in mind'. In which case, when Brown says that argument A assumes or presupposes P, we may charitably suppose he really means:

    Argument A is invalid
    Argument B = (A+P) is valid
So Smith in propounding A was assuming B

VII.37 Principles and premisses

This analysis relies rather heavily on charity. But life is too short for us to be always exchanging complete, exhaustively stated textbook arguments. If a point seems obvious or generally agreed we leave it out, prepared to defend it only if someone else should question it. Most of our reasoning life is spent proposing and receiving arguments with holes in, as we share with the rest of our argumentative society those unstated assumptions which if stated would complete our arguments.

Every argument works by some principle-of-inference. These are usually left unstated, being universally agreed; but they can be elicited and queried and set forth in capitals in logic-books:

Smith The greatest whole number cannot be odd, i.e. not even, for then adding 1 would produce a greater but an even one. Nor can it be even, by a similar argument. So no whole number is the greatest one.
Brown Your inference relies on the Excluded Middle principle. Please justify this presupposition, and proceed.

Principles of inference are of course difficult to justify, there being so little further back from which to start. But we can see that this sort of presupposition also founds two valid moods of inference:

    Principle P is unacceptable
    Argument A relies on principle P
So argument A is of uncertain force   (DC)

    Argument A is definitely O.K.
    Argument A relies on principle P
So principle P must be acceptable   (AA)

The latter mood, AA, is p-circular, since the principle would need confirming in the course of making sure the argument is O.K. But it might properly serve to dissuade a user of argument S from disowning P, its principle.

An assumption is a missing premiss: a principle is a rule directing or licensing an inference. These seem quite different, though both essential to reliable reasoning. An argument with insufficient premisses is bad in a different way from one with a faulty or missing principle of

VII.37 Principles and premisses

inference. Yet such a principle, once supplied, can be presented like an extra early premiss to the argument:

Brown   Jones is a bad man. He beats his wife.
Smith   You mean wife-beating is bad?
Brown   Jones beating Jones's wife is bad.
Robinson What about you and yours? You've no right to moral principles which just apply to Jones. If it's wrong for him it's wrong for anyone, at any time, with anybody's wife.

Here moral pressure is applied to 'universalize', i.e. to make quite general the principle of Brown's moral inference. A similar compulsion is applied in logic under the name 'parity of reasoning'.

When the principle is finally agreed it will not matter much whether we record it at the very beginning of the argument or off to one side as a rule governing the moves in this game (cp Carroll 1104).

The way in which principles of inference, or missing premisses, are taken for granted in an actual stated argument is comparable to the way in which subject-persons or facts are presumed to be available for reference, in actual statements: and to the way in which ingredient concepts are taken to be genuinely applicable by those who actually apply those other concepts in which they are ingredient.

38. DO PRESUPPOSITIONS MATTER?

These three logical relationships are not identical, but they have enough logical properties in common for all to bear the same name, unconfusingly. In particular, each of these three sorts of presupposition is detectable only on inspection of content, being an internal, non-functional relationship; and the propriety in question can be checked by inference only, from the presence or absence of the item presupposed. In each case, then, a Modus Tollens inference is quite in order, and is actually employed to check propriety, but a Modus Ponens argument from propriety back to the item presupposed is ultimately circular, as proof; though it can be used to discourage someone who does in fact make the

VII.38 Do presuppositions matter?

presupposition from also propounding a theory which involves denying it.

The argument back to referential presupposition was studied earlier, in the Cogito(#8f); that to conceptual presupposition was exemplified from Kant (#19f). Examples of backward argument from logical presupposition are not to hand, perhaps because their fallacy would be too obvious. But there is no telling what the future may produce.

Presupposition seems a purely linguistic relationship, connecting actual statements, concepts or arguments to the persons, ingredients or premisses they do or should contain. But these lnguistic relations are remarked on because they reflect underlying non-linguistic facts. In our communication-mode the assertion-unit 'Johnny won the race' presupposes that he ran in it. Now why is just this convention regarded as convenient? Because (by our race-conventions) winning a race involves running faster than the others in that race. Again, the statement 'Smith cross-examined Brown' is held to presuppose that Brown has already given evidence: not by a quirk of local idiom or legal prejudice, but just because legal proceedings go on in that way which our term 'cross-examine' was invented to describe. Thus the weight to be placed on a sound and non-circular argument from presupposition depends on the facts and arrangements in question, not just on the idioms locally employed for referring to those facts (cf #17 above).

Ought presuppositions always to be verified? If so, quite a slight remark will become a weighty catalogue. One will need to check that there is someone called George, that he does have a garden, and that he has planted peas in it, before daring to remark that George's peas are all in bloom. And perhaps one ought also to expound and analyse the concepts 'pea' and 'all' and 'bloom'?

That way madness lies. One would never get started on anything, as the concepts used in answering each prior question will have presuppositions of their own, in investigating which one would use further statements and concepts, with their presuppositions, needing to be checked, and so on (cp Griffiths 1955).

VII.38 Do presuppositions matter?

On the convention usually observed, speakers do take some things for granted. This saves time. It also enables them to make their points one at a time; an important matter, in speech, which is fleeting and serial. In order to say of George's peas just this one thing, that they are all in bloom, we must for the moment take-for-granted and leave almost unmentioned that host of essential preliminary but undisputed facts about the peas, the garden and the gardener (cp Palmer 1982).

Our language is so structured as to involve presupposition, in order that we may be able to say just one thing at a time. These presuppositions can usually be safely neglected. In everyday life prior questions normally need raising only if there is reason to think the answer will be negative. In the present discussion they are raised much more often, as our interest in presuppositions is mainly technical and argumentative (cp Kempson 49f).

Note D. What linguists do with 'presuppose'.

Presupposition has also been studied by linguists, as it affects their project of devising explicit rules to 'generate' each possible sentence of a given language and 'predict' its meaning from the meanings of the words in it (Cooper 125). If these latter, 'semantic' rules are truth-conditional than classical, two-valued logic is to hand to deal with them. If however the relation of presupposition is required in formulating some semantic rules, then a three-valued logic must be used. There are many such, still under construction, and inherently less definitive. So while some linguists favour using the notion of presupposition to help formulate adequate semantic rules, others are understandably anxious that its use may create more problems than it solves, and would prefer if possible to get by without (cp Atlas 1978, Wilson 3f).

Presupposition has been called on mainly to explain what is suggested but not actually said:

```
The King of France is bald    (France a monarchy)
John regrets going home       (he did go)
George got up and dressed     (in that order)
```

Linguists who prefer their logic two-valued will seek other ways to 'predict' these suggestions, e.g. by a separate sub-theory of speakers' intentions and context or circumstance, with presuppositions then located in this 'pragmatic' area (Kempson 137f; cp Grice 1961, 1981, Stalnaker 1974, Schwarz 1977, Caton 1981).

Another approach is to admit presupposition as a logical relationship but distinguish it from pragmatic constraints on the point and content of particular remarks. Logical presuppositions (there is a King of France) are then dealt with separately and differently from speaker-presuppositions (other things he had in mind - e.g. that you care who is and is not bald).

Chapter Eight

BACKWARD MOVES IN CURRENT DEBATE

The relations of presupposition, just reviewed, underly a surprising number of moves in current philosophical debate: surprising, because the relations themselves are often not distinctly recognized, but lumped in with others which are more familiar. The inferences which turn on them are not in consequence seen to form a class. In fact, there is a whole spectrum of inferential matter, from simple slogans up to full-blown transcendental arguments, all of which move 'back' from presupposing statement to item presupposed, and all of which are subject to the limitations we have noted for such inference: that they can serve in refutation only, not as proof, for fear of p-circularity.

This claim can be made good only by citing instances, so there follows an assortment of familiar topics of debate, analysed along the lines expounded earlier. The topics themselves are miscellaneous, but they share a common logical structure: they all rely (in fact) on presupposition, and propose some form of inference from it.

Our comments on these instances will be formal and, by now, predictable. We are not trying to decide what ought to be done with all these arguments, but only to show that anyone taking such decisions had better take account of their peculiar 'backward' character.

The general point is this: there is a specially close 'internal' relation between S and P, if S presupposes P; which means that the propriety of saying S cannot be made out while P is still in

106

doubt. In consequence, the minor premiss 'but S' may not be asserted in the course of proving something presupposed by it.

39. PRESUPPOSES, NOT IMPLIES

Many attempts have been made to reduce 'presupposes' to 'implies'; so as to make life easier for analysts, and also by way of defending the claim that certain two-valued calculi are adequate to express all logical relationships. It was shown above that these attempts must fail (#32). We now show how some simple debating moves have been mis-stated, in consequence of those attempts.

(a) <u>Impossible Duties.</u> It is not Smith's duty to do something that he cannot do; hence the slogan 'Ought implies Can'. This should read 'Ought presupposes Can'.

Take for example Smith's obvious duty to see his widowed mother comfortable. Wishing to increase his resources for doing this, he puts them on a hot tip for the National, which drops out halfway round the course. It can hardly be said that Smith's list of duties changed just when the horse began to walk. Why should mother-support become less obligatory out on a race-course, quite suddenly? Yet clearly there was from then on no point in discussing how Smith's resources 'ought' to be shared out, as he now had none. It is the statement 'Smith ought to see his mother comfortable', not the duty, that presupposes that he is in funds, and therefore 'can'.

We can still argue quite reliably from lack of an ability to absence of a duty, in fulfilling which that ability would be required: illiterates can't be expected to read notices, men should not be exhorted to bear children or to refrain from doing so.

This last illustration brings out a further difference between 'imply' and 'presuppose': if A implies B, then denying B involves denying A; but where S presupposes P the absence of P will make both S and its negation inappropriate. Thus consider Jones, an anti-feminist historian, who is scheming to murder good Queen Anne. That sounds uncivilized, we feel, almost treasonable. But we cannot now say 'Jones ought not to do it', for Queen Anne is dead. 'Ought not' also presupposes 'Can'.

VIII.39 Presupposes, not implies

Can we also argue back from the fact of duty to the ability which that duty would require? Kant is often credited with such an argument:

> We feel we really ought to do X; not for the sake of anything else, we just Ought. But if we couldn't do X, it couldn't be said that we Ought. Moreover 'doing' means doing-from-choice, which requires our being free to choose. So, as we recognize that we really ought-to-do X it must be the case that we are free-to-choose-to-do X, whatever science may tell us to the contrary.

This is a most encouraging argument, but it will not do. Categorical Imperatives should indeed be addressed to free agents, as it is no good addressing them to robots or to slaves. But a suitable recipient is part of a (properly-addressed) Imperative, so we can't make sure the Imperative is properly addressed while still checking out the recipient for suitability.

Suppose Joan is unsure if its a free agent that she is. Suppose also she seems to be hearing what - if its a free agent that she was - would be properly dubbed a Categorical Imperative, e.g. LOVE MY DOG. These two doubts do not cancel each other, and cannot be cobbled together by Kantian gobbledegook to make a certainty. Though it would be rather contrary of Joan to admit that she 'ought' to love my dog while still denying that she could. For no-one could reasonably think she was acting and also and consistently think she was compelled (cp Paton 217, Williams 100f).

Did Kant hope to prove Freedom from Duty, or just to remind us that Duty cannot be recognized without? It is now very hard to say. But we can say, now, that one inference is sound and the other circular.

(b) <u>Infallible Knowledge.</u> Only the truth can properly be 'known'. If Jill says she knows the door is shut and then finds it open she may not say 'I knew, but I was wrong'. Knowledge, then, must be infallible, once it is acquired. So anything which even might be wrong cannot possibly be known. Knowledge is to be had only of things that are unchangeable ... (cf Evans 129f, Harrison 1979).

VIII.39 Presupposes, not implies

For these arguments to work, Jill's remark must be held to imply that the door is shut, so that its being open after all will make her statement **false**. This seems a little hard on Jill.

'Jill knows X' means that correct information on that topic is in Jill's possession, and (usually) that she is aware of this. One item in this package is, that Jill's information is correct. Yet if Jack says Jill knows X, he is not currently saying that her information is correct, being much too busy saying that she has this (correct) information. The correctness is presupposed, and not implied, in Jack's remark; which means that remark is improper, not false, if Jill's information should turn out incorrect. From 'X is wrong' it only follows that 'one may not say that Jill knew X'. This inference Denies the Consequent of a referential presupposition, and is quite reliable.

The argument that true knowledge is infallible Affirms the Antecedent, and moves 'back' to what is presupposed. It will not, therefore, do for proving anything, since you would have to show first that your information was correct, to make sure that your knowledge-claim was appropriate, so as finally to 'infer' that your information was correct.

(c) Counting and Comparing things. You can't count things, not just things quite in general, e.g. 'all the things in the room'. You can only count things of some given sort: sunspots, or solecisms, or sausages. For the operation of counting requires some well-defined set whose members can be paired off one by one against the numerals (Geach 38).

Things may be good for this or that, e.g. a kitchen knife may be poor at spreading butter but quite good for cutting vegetables: but nothing is plain good (or bad) full stop. Appraisal involves some end or standard or scale by which to rank the items considered good or bad.

This point applies more generally. You can compare John with Jane in respect of height or intelligence or punctuality, but you can't compare them 'simply', i.e. in no particular respect. Every comparison presupposes some 'basis', some common aspect or feature, some dimension at least in which to go comparing John and Jane (cp Smith 1965).

VIII.39 Presupposes, not implies

These arguments show that things can be counted, valued or compared only as so-and-so's. Unless some class / purpose / feature is specified (or taken for granted) you can't count / value / compare those things. From this we may rightly infer, forwards, that where such specification is not to hand, the proposed counting / valuing / comparing is actually meaningless.

Someone might argue that, look, we do count / value / compare certain things, so there must be an underlying specification (perhaps a very very general one) of the 'things' concerned. Such an inference may be good as admonition but it will not do as proof. But no-one does offer such an argument as proof that the items in question have been specified: perhaps because in this case the circularity would be too obvious.

*   *   *   *

In each of these debating moves an item which in fact presupposes another item has been represented as implying it. As we saw, these two relationships are quite distinct (#32). The differences between them have affected the course of these debates; so these topics will now need to be re-worked.

40. 'AS IS' OR 'AS DESCRIBED'?

One reason why 'I think' presupposes an I is that in our language all doings require do-ers to be doing them. Is this need for subjects a very general fact about our world, which our language, not unnaturally, reflects? Or is it a fact just about our language, purely grammatical? Until that point is settled we cannot safely reason from the fact of thought to the subject which our word for it requires (cp #17 above).

(a) What appears?   Kant says we cannot know what things are really like but only how they seem to us; but we can still think of Things-as-they-really-are, and rest assured that some such Things must be, since how else could there be these Appearances, if there were nothing to appear? (B xxvii)

Yes indeed, if Smith calls X a shadow then Smith will have to grant some substance, Y, for X to

VIII.40 'As is' or 'as described'?

be a shadow of. But Brown need not grant that substance just because it's a shadow that Smith is calling X.

To argue that there must be Real Things upstairs, though quite unknown to us, since herebelow we meet with 'their appearances', is to rely on that description before arriving at the facts it was intended to describe. From the linguistic premiss that earthly things and processes are called 'phenomena' it does follow that their heavenly originals, if any, could well be <u>called</u> Real Things, Substances, Absolutes or Ultimates. It does not follow that there <u>are</u> such Things, or that they are different from phenomena. And much of the time Kant only intends the former, sounder inference: he just wants a way to speak of Ultimates - if such there be (cp B 294f).

(b) <u>Looking for Nessie.</u> Rudolf Otto thought we had a specifically religious 'sense' by which now and then we may come to feel a Presence, awful yet benign; a Wholly Other, fascinating, mysterious and terrible.

At some point in this quest evocation will give way to inference: you know that funny feeling as of such-and-such- a-one, well, if you have that feeling then there must <u>be</u> He or She or It. This inference turns on referential presupposition, of a special sort:

'A sense of X' presupposes X
I have a sense of X
So, there is an X.

Yes indeed, a sense of a mysterious presence does presuppose a mysterious Presence for it to be a sense of; or else that description of that sense would be inappropriate. But to infer the Presence from the sense-of-it one would need to know first that that sense was duly so described. Was it a sense of some particular Other, or a sense as of another, Other-ish? The answer, if we can find it, will decide whether our first description was approriate; but we cannot employ that propriety in divining that answer, as we do not have it <u>first</u>.

There is a similar line of encouragement regarding Truth. People spend their lives searching for Truth in this field or that. Their search

VIII.40 'As is' or 'as described'?

presupposes an object; if there were no such thing as Truth, how come they were looking for it all this time? But they do so look, in every clime and age, a noble, valiant company. Therefore, there is Truth.

Looking-for-X is indeed usually done with the aim of finding X: and if X is not then X will surely not be found, and looking-for-X will lose its usual point. However, if we are uncertain whether X exists, then maybe the only way to find out is to look for it. So a search-for-X which fails to find an X which was not there is quite successful, in its way. An expedition which does not find the Loch Ness Monster need not be ridiculous. But it is ridiculous to argue from the fact of the expedition - from people looking for Nessie - to Nessie being there.

(c) Theory-laden terms. Most theories bring along their own terminology, use of which will more or less commit the user to that theory. Thus an astronomer who speaks of 'the orbits of the planets round the sun' may not go on to deny that those apparently irregular stars do move in regular recurrent paths. The newsreader who speaks of 'a depression moving in from the Atlantic' is conceding thereby a complex theory about linking up places where the atmospheric pressure is the same, the resulting contours lying in concentric circuits of gradually increasing pressure, and the whole pattern then moving as a gradually changing whole across the map, etc etc. The newsreader, who is specially trained at reading things convincingly, may not realize all this until the weatherman points it out to him: "that forecast you read presupposes that places registering the same pressure do form concentric circuits, etc etc , and you will have to go along with that theory or else give up referring to depressions moving in".

This argument 'denies the consequent': rejection of the theory would make it inappropriate to speak of 'depression', a theory-laden term. This argument is sound, though perhaps a little hard on newsreaders.

When we have lived and worked a long time with a certain theory we may come to regard its technical terms as plain unvarnished descriptions of simple given fact, and might then take someone's apparently

VIII.40 'As is' or 'as described'?

successful reference to depressions or planetary orbits as evidence for the theories on which those descriptions did depend: "how could these forecasters swop their depression-stories, did not isobars join up in concentric circuits, etc etc ?" This argument works back to a presupposition, and ought not to convince.

Patrick, out for the day in the country, asks his atheist friend David where all the creatures could come from, if no Creator were responsible. David says they are not creatures to him, but only animals: rejecting the term, its presupposition, and the argument. For the argument was verbal only, and words do not determine facts.

*   *   *   *

We cannot determine how things are by inference from how they are described; at most, we can in that way confirm the coherence of our various descriptive terms and theories. In particular, we may want to establish the 'order of introduction' for the terms in some given theory; which task an argument from presupposition is fitted to achieve. Thus one could urge that the notion of comparison was not obtained by abstraction from a practice of comparing things, since any such comparing would presuppose a respect in which comparison is made, and this in turn presupposes the notion of comparison. Kant argues along such lines that our ideas of Space and Time are not empirical (B 38,46). The argument is purely negative; and we may find it applies equally to alternative theories. If Reality contains both chickens and eggs philosophers cannot alter this set-up by proving both orders of priority between them to be equally illogical.

41. BRICKS AND STRAW

If B is an element in A, or a stage along our way to A, and if A cannot be arrived at except by means of B, then B is 'essential' to our having A, i.e. if we don't have B then we can't have A. Arguments to this effect are easy to construct but less easy to evaluate: how can we make sure that B is the only way to get to A? And if it is, how may that limit our deployment of the argument?

VIII.41 Bricks and straw

(a) <u>Too good to be true.</u> Television helps us all enjoy our weather more. At the first wintry shower we can see juggernauts stranded in hedge-high drifts of snow, with helicopters dropping hay to sheep and bread to isolated villagers, and feel there is just chaos everywhere. The social purpose of these clips is understandable: to get some viewers to leave their cars at home. But the more thoughtful may remark that a team of photographers had to get out there on the moors, by car, to take those photographs, and then bring the film back down to town again for processing. If the story which those pictures tell were true then we could not be viewing them. Their untruth is thus established 'transcendentally', by reference to 'what makes viewing possible'.

Another popular topic, with some children and most parents, is the unfairness of exams. A ready welcome awaits the researcher who shows yet again that class tests or A-level grades do not really measure the pupils' ability or diligence. Does this mean the researcher has some better measure of these things, by which to show our everyday gradings are inaccurate? It is no good checking my watch by yours unless there is reason to think that yours is right. And without some such yardstick, independent and superior, the most any educationist can ever show is that existing tests do not always give the same results.

In both these cases, the initial 'face value' of a statement may be somewhat qualified by reflection on the conditions necessary for making it.

(b) <u>Branch-cutting.</u> We are sometimes told we have no right to such-and-such a concept till we have 'given an account of it', i.e. said just what it is and how we came by it. Berkeley wanted 'matter' to be justified like this, or thrown away. Hume put a similar question-mark against 'cause' and 'thing' and 'individual'. Now some such calls to "stand and deliver" admit of a telling personal reply: Your challenge presupposes the very concept you are questioning. You are for cutting off the branch on which you sit. For example, it needs a continuing identical Hume to raise Hume's ongoing doubts about personal identity. The reader had better be persevering too, for Hume's doubts are difficult to follow and several pages long.

Some concepts are hard to explain because no definition covers every case: thus if religion be reckoned as 'worship of a god or gods' that will leave out Buddhism and the Jains, but if we take it as just a way of life that might let in Marxism and even Rotary. Should we then give up the term altogether, until a foolproof definition is devised? Not so, for the conclusion that we do not know what religion is at all would prevent us from saying that Buddhism is one and Marxism is not: our undermining of the definitions would thus itself be undermined.

Socrates used to test definitions by whether they fitted the admitted instances, and sometimes ended by discarding all the received accounts as inadequate: the accounts, not the concept they were failing to define. So his conclusion did not invite the riposte "But look what you are sitting on!"

(c) <u>Not in front of the children.</u> Some say there is no such thing as morality. They grant that people do talk 'morally', for certain purposes, but deny that this moral terminology has any reference to real qualities or genuine relationships. Not but what mugs who wrongly think it does may still be gulled into adjusting their behaviour, by a suitable use of 'moral' terminology.

Is this story coherent? Or has the cynic been forced to grant the morality he was trying to expose?

The cynic may well suppose that some people will blunder on with the exploded old morality, imagining that killing is 'wrong' and that health is somehow 'good'. And certainly the cynic's exposure presupposes their error, i.e. if they didn't make it he would have nothing to explode. But his account of moral terms as official humbug put about by interested governors does not presuppose the 'morality' they peddle or assume it genuine or true — not until his righteous indignation betrays him into calling their humbug wicked, deceitful, selfish and conscienceless.

The ordinary man who can't or won't follow the cynic's account, but just soldiers on, does indeed take for granted the morality the cynic is trying to explode: and thus enables others to influence his actions by their 'deceitful' use of moral terms. And the cynic, in explaining this, must assume that

VIII.41 Bricks and straw

that is how 'moral' people will react to certain words. But their morality is not presupposed as true in his explanation, which does not even assume that moral terms make sense. He is only setting out a system some people have, for using them, for certain purposes.

As people come to accept the cynic's account they will presumably turn a deafer ear to moral blame and praise, thus reducing the stock of 'ordinary' people for humbuggers to manipulate. And this may make it unwise for the cynic to go on explaining things to everyone: certainly those in charge would be unwise to let him go on doing so. For enlightened ex-mugs, who now see that 'justice' only means 'the rulers' interest' may well not put themselves out any more in furthering that interest, where it is to their own detriment (cp Plato 15f).

There are, then, good cynical reasons for silencing a cynic like Thrasymachus. But not logical ones. He has not presupposed the logic he was trying to explode. He is sawing, all right, but then he isn't on that branch.

*   *   *   *

If B is essential to our having A, yet somehow conflicts with A, then there must be something wrong with A: the snowdrifts we see cannot be the whole story, examination results cannot in this way be shown non-significant. The demand for definition is over-stated, if concepts as yet undefined are used in the process of rejecting one.

These arguments from presupposition merely disable an argument or picture, without replacing it or supporting an alternative. The disabling works, if B is really shown essential to our having A: in the case of the moral cynic that presupposition was not established, so the refutation fails.

**   **   **   **

The arguments touched on in this chapter all turn on presupposition, though this has not been generally recognized; and they have often been wrongly assessed, in consequence. Those in the next chapter are more obviously 'transcendental' in structure and intent, and exhibit more clearly the transcendental fallacy.

Chapter Nine

METAPHYSICAL RESEARCH

Several major lines of enquiry into the ultimate nature of things have proceeded by means of backward arguments. In some cases the arguments are now quite generally held to be unsound, though the reason may not be so clearly recognized. And as 'metaphysics' is frequently dismissed as mere speculation, some of the old arguments are now being re-packaged as 'conceptual analysis'.

42. WHICH COMES FIRST?

Which things in our world are more basic, simple and fundamental, and which are complex, constructed and derivative? Their Maker did not label them for us. But we may be able to sort some of them out by abstract argument, reasoning that items of type B <u>could not occur</u> in a world not equipped with items of type A: no army without soldiers; no fraud without money; no sentences if there are no words ... Items of type A, then must have ontological priority. They are more basic, overall.

(a) <u>Metaphysical priority.</u> According to Locke and his followers all our knowledge must at first have come from the itemized personal experiences each of us separately is alleged to have. From such 'impressions of the senses' you and I must have built up those generalized complex notions of each other and of people, things and processes, which we later name and so manage to converse about.

Experiences come first, on this account; particular, personal, private episodes of acquaintance with Reality. Public people and

IX.42 Which comes first?

material things come a long time afterwards. Now this account would collapse if it could be shown that people are prior to such atomized experience:

> These alleged items of separate personal experience all need to be identified, for we must know whom we are referring to, when assembling them into more complex notions, or when constructing these graphic accounts of our supposedly Meccano-like learning processes. Now a private experience of Robinson's, e.g. a toothache, can be identified by Smith and referred to only as a toothache 'felt by Robinson'.

The suggestion is not that Robinson can't have a toothache until Smith feels able to refer to it; but rather, that Smith can refer to 'it' or indeed think of 'it' only as somebody's, i.e. Robinson's; and that Robinson himself could conceive it only in this way. In which case Robinson's toothache presupposes Robinson, so an account in which the toothache comes <u>first</u> cannot be correct.

Why can Smith refer to Robinson's toothache only in that possessive way, as a toothache 'had' by Robinson? Partly because to our way of thinking an experience needs an experiencer, as a thought needs a thinker to be thinking it. But Buddhists might reject this requirement, since they deny the soul or Self. Should we then say that thoughts need thinkers <u>in our local mode of speech</u>? In that case the priority of persons to toothaches may be conceptual only, and parochial, not real, general and 'metaphysical' (cp Kolb 1975).

We could still say that a metaphysical scheme in which individual sense-experiences are the basic entities is not natural to our language as it is, so that continual care and constant qualification may be needed, for expressing it. But then most metaphysical schemes are meant to reform our ways of talking and thinking of the world. That is why books on the topic quite commonly appear difficult.

(b) <u>Too much hangs thereby.</u> In a well-articulated deductive system all the theorems are shown to follow from the axioms or principles. So one may ask what right we have to rely upon those principles. It is no use proving them by some

IX.42 Which comes first?

further and more fundamental principles, for that would only move the question one stage further back. So why not turn the argument around:

> Consider these theorems, how important, how certain, how well-known! But they all presuppose these principles. How could you deny those, since you must then abandon all these theorems?

The theorems do not exactly presuppose, but rather follow from the principles. And these may not be the only principles they would follow from; perhaps there are other axiom-sets from which the same body of theorems could be deduced. So we cannot argue back from these theorems, however grand, to just those principles. And in any case such an argument seems pleasantly inconsequent, for surely our trust in the theorems is based on our having deduced them from those principles!

In the case of principles of inference, which are taken for granted each time they are applied, we may well be impressed by the extent of the havoc their abandonment would wreak:

> The Laws of Thought reduce to one principle, the systematic nature of thought and things. Though unprovable, this is sufficiently guaranteed by the fact that if it were denied, it would be impossible to know or prove anything (Latta + 116).

Suppose we grant that the system, S, of Aristotelian logic does presuppose some principle, P, as the nerve of all its argument. Then, if P be not granted, S may not be proclaimed. In this situation, someone who wants logic and thinks only this one is available is going to grant P, just as a bank clerk threatened with a shotgun will be sensible to make some funds available. Logical justification is a different affair.

Such an arrangement is sometimes said to justify S by the 'systematically disastrous' results of not having P. This description is correct: but the disaster affects the system, not the items it contains. We might have to say goodbye to Euclid, but not to cones and parallelograms. The lack of a presupposition can only affect our way of thinking or talking or arguing, and that may of course affect

IX.42 Which comes first?

our other ways of dealing with things, but not the things we deal with.

The argument that 'too much hangs thereby' is already familiar, from Kant. He rightly thought that geometry 'as he knew it' could not survive the denial that Space and Time are our contribution to Experience. As a result, geometry underwent a subtle but far-reaching change: it was freed from immediate reference or 'application' to worldly things. Thus the 'systematically disastrous' result of that denial was not the justification of geometry as Kant and his age all 'knew' it, but a major revision of the idea and nature of geometry(cp #24).

*   *   *   *

An argument about the 'order of introduction' of concepts in our scheme cannot settle the order or dependence of the Real Things they were meant to comprehend. At most it can show certain theories inconsistent with the scheme used in formulating them: much as 'sunrise' and 'sunset' might be used in a first determination of time in a system of astronomy which when fully developed discards these terms as metaphorical and inappropriate.

An argument that 'too much hangs thereby' can at most show the order of proof in some given system. Displaying the order of reasoning will not justify the starting-points, nor further establish the conclusions - except by showing these as derived from those.

43. REFUTING REDUCTIONS

Reductions and other definitional accounts can sometimes be refuted by showing that the term defined or disposed of is actually presupposed in the account which was meant to render it dispensable. Thus if someone set out to reduce morality to the requirements of society, so that strictly moral judgments would become dispensable, this proposal may be countered by showing that the social requirement in question could not be adequately stated without using moral terms.

IX.43 Refuting reductions

(a) **People aren't disposable.** Some people say that a person is **just** so many atoms or cells. So talk about people should be replaceable by talk about sets and structures of atoms and cells; which suggests that people are not so very basic in the real scheme of things. A linguistic reduction thus serves as springboard for a metaphysical advance.

This move could be blocked by showing that the proposed reduction will not work, because some statements about people are not translatable without loss into terms purely physical or biological, for example because those statements would themselves require people, to be making them.

This refutation makes appeal to presupposition: B presupposes A, so you can't have a scheme containing B but lacking A, so you can't keep B while discarding A; therefore A's cannot be reduced to B's. Now this conclusion is language-relative: **in our conceptual scheme** A's are not reducible to B's. But the proposed reduction also was language-relative; so the refutation stands. If however the refutation were to fail, and the reduction went through, we should all be tempted to move from 'term A is dispensable' to 'A's are non-fundamental things'; a bold leap across into metaphysics, which leaves sound reasoning behind.

(b) **Knowledge requires truth.** An emotive theory of ethics is sometimes regarded as merely inconsequent:

> It is impossible to approve of anything without thinking it **worthy** of approval - without thinking that it has a goodness of its own which makes it fit to be approved ... if things were only approved, without anything being worthy of approval, the act of approval would simply be nonsensical (Ross 261, cp Strawson 1949).

'Approve' is here taken as 'commend for its good qualities'; so 'good' may not in its turn be explained as 'commendable'. Half-hearted emotivism is thus shown inexpressible. But there is a full-blooded version too: that there is no such thing as goodness, though we may use the word 'good' to indicate our liking for some things. This full-blooded theory will involve redefining our 'ethical' terms, including their inter-relationships.

IX.43 Refuting reductions

Does my feeling obliged presuppose an Obligation for me to feel? No, for sometimes I feel obliged mistakenly. But yes, verbally it does: that particular description of my state of mind does require some 'object', some direction in which my feeling-obliged was felt to be aligned or aimed. So my feeling-obliged, if <u>properly</u> indulged and <u>correctly</u> so described, does presuppose some Object, some Obligation out there in the real world for me to feel constrained and obligated by. And by the time those underlined conditions have been securely fulfilled there will be nothing substantial left for such an argument to prove, but only the merely verbal point that there must be some obligation for me to feel, when I feel obliged.

Bishop Butler argues like this against the view that your personal identity could depend upon your realizing it:

> It is self-evident, that consciousness of personal identity presupposes and therefore cannot constitute personal identity, any more than knowledge, in any other case, can constitute truth, which it presupposes (<u>Identity</u> #4).

That seems fair. You can't define truth-about-X in terms of our knowledge-of-X; not without circularity. But is a corresponding account of identity absurdly circular? (cp Mackie 187)

Consider national identity. On one plausible account people become a nation just by thinking of themselves as one, and feeling they are all co-heirs to that national history. They may also think of their nation as some august invisible entity, almost a person: bearing a name, receiving oaths of loyalty, represented by a flag. These nationalist fictions are real, so far as they are thought and felt; and can be available to us <u>first</u>, as facts, when giving an account of national identity. It is only our description of them as 'national' (as in 'loyalty to the nation') that has to wait for our concept of 'nation' to emerge.

People are fictions, one might say: we exist because we make us up. If some thinker thinks himself continuous with some earlier one (e.g. Smith-yesterday), taking on all his thoughts and memories and responsibilities, then a case of

IX.43 Refuting reductions

personal identity may be happening. This is surely not the whole story, or the only story, and it may not even be the most convincing one, but it does make sense. So Butler's refutation was too quick. He rests too much upon a genitive.

The phrase 'the top of the hill' does presuppose a hill, to be top of: the hill may not be explained in terms of what it was leading up to. But 'a feeling of anger' is not an anger with a feeling tagging on to it, but a feeling suitably delimited and qualified: an arrangement we should never make out if we argued from the 'of'. So we cannot safely infer, in some disputed case, such as 'a consciousness of identity', that the identity it indubitably presupposes had to be there <u>first</u>, for it to be a consciousness of.

(c) <u>What bodies are made of.</u> Hume offered to refute the 'modern philosophy' of Locke by a single 'very decisive objection', based on presupposition. For Locke, colours, tastes and sounds are just perceptions, nothing more: though we do see colours, the things we see are not really coloured, for colour is something that happens in the process of our seeing things. But the idea of motion, Hume replies, "necessarily presupposes that of a body moving", and the idea of a moving body "must resolve itself into the idea of extension, or of solidity", and so on until we come to perceptual atoms, which must be perceived as coloured or as tangible. So if colour were unreal the whole chain of perceptual constructs would disappear (I.2 #3, 4 #4).

Hume's chain of presuppositions goes like this:

1. Motion presupposes body, for only bodies move.
2. Body reduces to extension and solidity.
3. Extension must consist of points.
4. Points can be perceived only as coloured or as tangible.
5. If colour is unreal, coloured points cannot make up real things.
6. Tangibility is a property of bodies.
7. (return to 2)

Conclusion: Any account of 'body', on this theory, is impossible, so the theory must be wrong.

IX.43 Refuting reductions

The first three links in this inference propose conceptual analyses, which may be quite correct. The fourth, however, makes a general observation about how human beings come across points, in their experience. This difference destroys the alleged circle of analysis.

Research into perceptual origins is not easily combined with conceptual analysis, as the methods are wholly different. In particular: doing something may not always require, in the doer, all the concepts that would be required for doing it:

> Smith is busy learning this and that 'by the way of ideas, as he comes across them in experience: impression first, then idea, xeroxed for filing; class and name a long time afterwards. Smith's ideas do not come to him labelled, he has to sort them out and label them. Robinson, a philosophical novelist, is watching Smith at work, from a novelist's know-all inside-outside vantage point. Robinson 'sees' Smith see and touch a point, and is writing up what Smith has made of the experience. For this purpose, Robinson must have mastered a suitable sub-system of concepts, such as 'touch', body' and 'solidity'. But Smith does not now require all this apparatus of ideas, for he is not describing anything, he is just having the experience.

Of course, for Smith to see the points he must in some sense experience what Robinson calls 'colour' and 'solidity'. But he need not name or think of them like that, not having as yet mastered the linguistic and conceptual system he is still struggling to acquire (cp Myers 1978).

Grown-ups watching infants often comment on this point: the curiosity and wonder so plain on the face but not put into words, the learning which would never happen if the orderly requirements of language and grammar were enforced on disorderly experience. A similar point was made in the cover-cartoon of Potter's <u>Gamesmanship</u>: a golfer anatomized, with all his muscles displayed as he poised for a stroke, and the warning: Don't look at this, show it to your opponent.

IX.43 Refuting reductions

(d) <u>Conceptual nit-picking</u>. F.H.Bradley perfected a technique for rejecting goods by alleging faults in their conceptual packaging:

> A concept is nothing without its qualities, yet cannot <u>be</u> with them, not without a logician-proof account of 'with', yet this relation also is unintelligible, for "relation presupposes quality, and quality relation. Each can be something neither together with, nor apart from, the other: and the vicious circle in which they turn is not the truth about reality"(21).

So Space, Time, Motion, Activity and Things follow Quality and Relation into the metaphysician's reject bin. But we can hardly discover what does not exist by showing that our descriptions of it are not good enough.

An objection along similar lines is raised by Quine to the notion of analytic truth. Granting that 'all bachelors are unmarried' is permanently true just because 'bachelor' and 'unmarried man' are synonyms, you will still have 'synonym' to explain, and that will bring 'analytic' in again. Different circuits await us if we explain 'analytic' in terms of definitions, or of semantic rules. Since all such accounts are circular, we had better stop distinguishing analytic propositions from synthetic ones - and much better we shall feel for it (1951; cp Grice + 1956).

This complaint makes 'explain' the converse of 'define', and all definitions introductory. A term is 'introduced' by equating it with some constellation of previously acquired terms, as 'isobar' equals 'line joining points of equal pressure'. To explain or give an account of isobars we then simply cite this definition, by which that term was created and introduced.

Some systems of mathematics and logic are indeed constructed in this way. In such systems, a definition must not include anything explainable by means of the term being introduced: circularity undoes everything. It is also clear that not all the terms can be defined: there have to be some 'primitives'. But it is not clear that all concept-arrays are constructed in this way, nor that all definitions are introductory, nor even that all

IX.43 Refuting reductions

sorts of word-explanation are rendered vacuous by circularity (cp #55 below).

(e) Robots keep out. Some people say everything is fixed. Every movement, every action, every thought results by strict rules from whatever went before. So everything we say and do is really determined in advance, and is 'in principle' predictable.

The people who say this are, presumably, commending these ideas to everyone, as being true. But the theory says we are robots. How could a robot assess an idea as being 'true'? Assessing an idea as true always involves comparing it with the contrary, and choosing one of them. But robots cannot choose: their 'selections' are determined in advance, programmed into them. Indeed, if this theory were correct no ideas could be commended either. Even assertion would be impossible. Not even language could occur. So, if mechanism were true, no-one could ever be asserting it, so if anyone does assert it, it has to be untrue. Only silence could be taken for consent (Malcolm 1968).

This refutation depends on our present understanding of terms, built up in a society in which free choice was assumed. A robot's language would clearly require to be different. Determinists (the human ones) have to live in our world and describe in our terms that other world to which, they believe, we all belong. It is no surprise that occasional inconcinnities result. The task for determinists is to create a new language, compatible with their theory yet accessible to us, and to get us to start talking it. They are busy with this project, and Malcolm's argument does show that they have still some way to go. To show that their project is impossible can only be done by assuming at the outset that our language is the only one, that linguistic change cannot happen because it would seem contradictory. It is not clear whether Malcolm intended to assume all that.

*   *   *   *

IX.43 Refuting reductions

A refutation is an attack on someone else's view or argument. To refute by presupposition is, to bring out some fatal incoherence in that view or argument: e.g. that if it were correct then that person could not hold that view or propound that argument.

A successful refutation simply returns us to Square One. It does not show how the facts or reasons really lie, nor even how they don't lie; it only shows that certain formulations or descriptions of them are inconsequent. A refutation is thus mainly about the language or conceptual scheme in which certain views or arguments are put. It shows us around the telescope, a bit, but not around the galaxy.

44. DESCRIPTIVE METAPHYSICS

Both Kant and Descartes expected to show something about the world at large, by their transcendental arguments: to display at least in outline how things really were, or failing that to make out why they should seem to us the way they always do.

Similar arguments have again been advanced quite recently, and with similar intent. The new transcendentalists hope, of course, to avoid their predecessors' fallacies, but still expect to achieve by argument an improved overall account of how things really are. Their arguments also work back from something being presupposed, and suffer, though perhaps less obviously, from the drawbacks inherent in all backward argument. We look first at a minor instance from quite another field, which may bring out the 'hopeful' nature of such inference.

(a) It's got to be stopped. A recent judgment by Lord Denning displays some transcendental tendencies. The case was thus: an electricity Board surveying possible sites for nuclear power stations was obstructed by locals who did not want one there. The police declined to intervene because the obstruction was on private land and no violence was used. The Board asked the Court to tell the police to help. The case turned on whether such obstruction could properly be termed a 'breach of the peace':

127

IX.44 Descriptive metaphysics

> Every person who was prevented from carrying out his lawful pursuits was entitled to use self-help. He must not use more force than was reasonably necessary but there was no doubt that he could use force to do it. Further, the conduct of these people, their criminal obstruction, was itself a breach of the peace ... if someone unlawfully and physically obstructed the worker, by tying down or chaining himself to the rig or the like, he was guilty of a breach of the peace ... If there was no breach of the peace nor apprehension of it, it would give a licence to every obstructor and passive resister in the land. He would be able to cock a snook at the law as these groups had done. Public works of the greatest national importance could be held up indefinitely. That could not be: the rule of law had to prevail (Denning 1981).

There must be some rules, says the Judge, if life is to go on: and those rules must be able to rule out any activities which, if pursued, could prevent our life going on in its accustomed way. So the 'rule of law' must be held to make it actually unlawful for people to go round obstructing lawful survey work, however much disliked, however peacefully.

These are powerful persuasions, of a sort often met with in <u>Hansard</u> or in the leader columns of <u>The Times</u>, to commend some change in the existing law. But here they are reported as part of a judgment in court, directed to declaring what the law now is or must be deemed to be.

Some deeming is bound to go on, in this process, in difficult cases with conflicting precedents. This deemster, unwisely perhaps, has given us his reasoning:

1. Life under the rule of law presupposes laws adequate to inhibit activity destructive of that life.
2. Obstructing official survey work could have some such destructive tendency.

So 3. existing legal provisions, e.g. those regarding 'breach of the peace', must be construed in a way that will illegalize obstruction of that sort.

IX.44 Descriptive metaphysics

To the non-legal mind, this is wishful arguing. If judges can deem anything illegal under Rule 42, just because they think 'there ought to be law against it', then it is goodbye to the rule of law, no citizen is safe, and we have no need for Parliament.

(b) <u>Indispensable individuals</u>. P.F.Strawson begins a long argument with the fact that we do refer to people and to things; and refer successfully, for when Smith mentions Brown, Robinson can usually make out whom he is referring to. Strawson has his own theory of how this must be done; a theory which if true will confound the sceptic whose questions and denials are so destructive of intellectual society.

One such question is this: when can I rightly be sure that that's the <u>same</u> table, decanter or toothbrush that I saw last night? The very same one, not just one that is extremely similar. Well, says Strawson, if we never were sure, and if in consequence we never did call this or that the same would start each time our observation got switched on: New Every Morning - not just the love our wakening and uprising prove, but the bed we rise from, the floor we stand on, the room, the street plan, Space itself, a complete new Universe after each and every blink. Saturday night and Sunday morning might indeed show many similarities, but we could not on Sunday regard these as left over from the night before, as we should have no basis for comparison. But we do in fact question if that toothbrush is the same, or a different one, and

> such a doubt makes sense only if the two systems are not independent, if they are parts, in some way related, of a single system which includes them both. But the condition of having such a system is precisely the condition that there should be satisfiable and commonly satisfied criteria for the identity of at least some items in one sub-system with some items in the other. This gives us a more profound characterization of the sceptic's position. He pretends to accept a conceptual scheme, but at the same time quietly rejects one of the conditions of its employment (35).

IX.44 Descriptive metaphysics

Strawson starts from "our idea of a single spatio-temporal system of material things": that is our conceptual scheme, and "we cannot change it even if we would". A condition, he claims, "of our having this conceptual scheme is the unquestioning acceptance of particular-identity in at least some cases of non-continuous observation."

This inference turns on conceptual presupposition, though he does not use that term:

1. The notion of all our separate perceptions being perceptions of one world presupposes that some items in one stretch of observation can be reckoned 'the same' as some in another,
2. We do have the notion of all our separate perceptions being perceptions of one world,

so 3. Some items in one stretch of observation can be identified with some in another, i.e. whatever may count as 'identifying' it must be a task we sometimes can achieve.

This argument cannot serve as proof that identifications do occur, for if that were in doubt we could not properly be said to have the notion of a single World. But it does help to locate such identifying in the constructive activity by which that World is made and is preserved; . and so makes identifying a respectable activity (cp Palmer 1966). And the argument will confute any one-world sceptic who denies our right ever to identify one perceived item with another; though such a peculiar stance is not, perhaps, to be inferred just from the sceptic's use of a language, e.g. English, in which One World seems to be normally assumed; for by that principle we should all be flat-earthers in astronomy. We need positive explicit statements, to show that our would-be sceptic really does 'accept the Universe'.

This argument, like Kant's, is good for confounding rather foolish sceptics with, but incompetent for proving that the World is One. It is linguistic in effect, i.e. it can only display conceptual structures, showing us around our spider's web (cp Smith 1974, Taylor 1979).

IX.44 Descriptive metaphysics

Strawson tries to meet this point, at the outset, by re-definition of a vital term:

> descriptive metaphysics is content to describe the actual structure of our thought about the world, revisionary metaphysics is concerned to produce a better structure (9).

His own work, he suggests, is only descriptive, non-revolutionary, factual. But this revisionary distinction does not correspond to any clear division in the facts he was attempting to describe. 'Metaphysics' has always referred to man's efforts to describe (ultimate) reality, so all metaphysics is descriptive, in intent at least. None is wholly successful: i.e. every metaphysic so far has mis-described the Universe, to some extent. Each fresh system of metaphysics is therefore an attempt to put right earlier mistakes: so all metaphysics is revisionary too (cp Allison 1969).

We may also decide to discuss these describings of reality: to consider the describers, their motives and interests, their equipment, and how well placed they are for viewing the objects they describe. In particular, we may reflect on their modes of expression and communication, linguistic and conceptual. Such reflection forms a part of the theory of knowledge, and could well be called 'linguistic philosophy' (cp Rorty 1978).

On this convention we would have to say that any conclusions drawn by means of Strawson's arguments will be 'linguistic' rather than 'metaphysical'. Yet his ultimate interest, like that of most abstract reasoners, is surely in how things ultimately <u>are</u>. He wants to say how the world is, or some corner of it anyway, and he wants to say it better than those who went before.

(c) <u>What just must be there.</u> Ross Harrison sets out to determine the essential features of the world, just by arguing. It must be comprehensible, for an enquiring philosopher can have no interest in any other sort. Comprehensibility presupposes three further features: that some distinction can be made between true and false judgments; that the world is temporal; that action is possible within the world. Harrison is mainly concerned to decide the order in which these features should be introduced, in the construction of his 'general model world', and to derive other subsidiary but necessary features from these. He is engaged in "an inquiry into the essential conditions of any world being a comprehensible one: or an inquiry into the fundamental features of any comprehensible conceptual scheme"(32). Our concern is with the formal structure of his argument:

1. To be intelligible, the world must be A,B,C,
2. The world, we must assume, is intelligible,
So 3. The world is A, B, C.

As a proof, this is inconsequent, for the assumption that the world is intelligible may not be made before knowing that it fulfils the conditions laid down therefor, namely being A and B and C. As a refutation, the argument may strike home: a sceptic who assumes that the world makes sense but then works round to denying A or B or C must have gone wrong somewhere, having cut off the branch that he was sitting on and sawing from.

That is always unwise, for you can't saw anything once your branch has gone. Whether it was a good branch to sit on in the first place, is a quite separate question. Maybe the world is intelligible and is A and B and C. Or maybe it does not make sense, but hides some mysterious Surd among its principles. The argument does nothing to establish or to disprove either alternataive.

(d) Ultimate moral principles. Some say you can't question all the principles of morality, as you would need to rely on some of them, in questioning.

One way to question principle X of morality is to commend another and contrary but equally moral principle Y; and clearly you cannot in this way question all moral principles at once. Another way to question a principle is to ask what good reasons there are, if any, for accepting it. Non-committal questioning of this sort could presumably be applied to all the principles of morality, as no moral principle is appealed to in such open-minded questioning. So thorough-going scepticism about morality seems feasible, if it be not dogmatic, but sceptically framed.

IX.44 Descriptive metaphysics

While such sceptical sceptics plainly do not require other moral principles as premises, for their questioning of principles, do they nevertheless rely in some other way on some such principles, in their activity of questioning?

One might question the principle that one ought to consider others ... the answer "*You* need not bother about anyone else" might possibly be correct. But giving such an answer depends on there being either a general presumption that one ought to bother about others ... or at least that there are rules governing what one ought to do. Unless there are such rules, one could have no idea what it was for it to be necessary to do something, and the expressions 'you must' and 'you need not' could have no use (Griffiths 1958).

So an agent with no rules of action would not use or need or understand an 'ought' and so could not even start on the sceptical enquiry as to whether one ought to considr others also, or just oneself. On this view the questioning of principle X presupposes some other principle, Z, to give sense to the moral terminology employed in such questioning.

What could be established, at best, by this line of reasoning? Suppose Smith is questioning principle X, i.e. enquiring how reliable it is. Robinson notes that Smith's questioning presupposes principle Z, i.e. such questioning would be out of place or senseless if Z were untrue or were not available to Smith. Now Robinson asks himself whether Smith's questioning really does make sense. To answer with rational confidence, Robinson must dig out all the items presupposed by Smith's would-be activity, and check on all of them, including Z. To argue that Z must be available because, look, Smith really is engaged in questioning, is pure Looking Glass reasoning.

All we can fairly conclude is that principle Z, if required to make sense of Smith's questioning, is not itself for the moment up for questioning by Smith. But being-unquestionable-now-for-Smith is not quite the same as being true.

IX.44 Descriptive metaphysics

There is nothing personal in this. It is not that Z may be questioned by Brown but not by Smith; rather, that anyone is debarred from questioning-Z-while-questioning-X. So even if some principle could be found presupposed by all sorts of moral questioning, that would only show that it was not open to question while questioning the other principles.

The defender of morality may now widen his appeal, to the 'moral language' in which moral claims are made and questioned and denied and even overlooked:

> A principle can be shown to be objectively true, without appealing to factors outside itself, if it can be shown that the form of discourse of which the principle is an example is impossible without presupposing the principle. That is, by showing that no-one can claim to be using a form of autonomous, practical and objective discourse unless he at the same time accepts the principle in question (Griffiths 1969).

This seems a very fruitful line of reasoning. Any arguer will have to talk or write his argument, and so can be held committed to the principles which that form of discourse is supposed to presuppose (cp Moulds 1972).

What principles? For Griffiths, any moral discussion demands Impartiality, Liberty and Rational Benevolence. These are required like rules of procedure. They are necessary conventions for the business of moral debate. And moral sceptics also are in that line of business (cp Peters 124).

Are they really? Is it a moral question, whether a moralist is speaking from knowledge or only from conviction? To take a parallel, while the question 'What is the square root of 25?' is clearly mathematical, the question 'Should square roots be taught in Middle School?' is educational in character. Likewise the question 'Are all moral principles open to question?', though moral in subject-matter is itself epistemological in character.

IX.44 Descriptive metaphysics

Now it could be argued that rational discussion of any topic whatever rests on certain moral principles, thus putting them beyond question for those taking part in the debate. To establish this view such discussion must be shown impossible for those who reject such underlying principles. It is not enough to show that a perfect discussion needs such perfect participants, or that the world would be a nicer place if only everyone agreed ... or even that participation in debates will generally be freer and more rewarding if all parties respect freedom, have generous motives, and are not partisan. For the fact is that many ordinary imperfect humans have quite second-rate sub-angelic discussions with their friends, and indeed their enemies: discussions which, no doubt, leave much to be desired, but which are nonetheless understood and set forward by their participants. Did they rely unavoidably on Impartiality, Liberty and Rational Benevolence? That still requires to be shown.

To prove that principle Z is unavoidably presupposed in form-of-discourse D, one must show the absence-of-Z making D impossible: not just unsatisfactory. Impossible for whom? If Smith uses form-of-discourse D, and Jones follows what Smith says, and convinces Smith of this by his replies, and they then have a D-discussion to their mutual pleasure and enlightenment, then outsiders like Robinson are poorly placed to rule out their discussion as impossible. Though he is of course free to explain once again to Smith and Jones and everyone just why the use of D must involve reliance on principle Z.

In these discussions of ours about Smith and Jones the terms 'nonsense' and 'impossible' really bear a special sense. No-one denies that astrologers do talk to each other, and appear to understand. Few will claim that books on Yoga are literally meaningless. When people describe these systems as nonsense or rubbish they mean that the occult forces connections and organs there referred to just do not exist, so that statements about them fail for lack of reference. Yet those statements are made and understood; indeed it is only by understanding them that one can make out their lack of reference.

IX.44 Descriptive metaphysics

Descartes argued from 'I think', and his argument seemed compelling just because that premiss was so general: what party to the debate can deny that he has ideas? The argument from moral discourse is only one degree less general: the debaters must just decide first that their debate is indeed a moral one. This requires some prior division of discourse into 'forms' or areas. But how can we decide just where to draw the line around morality, while we are still engaged in disputing moral principles (cp Palmer 1968, Phillips 1968).

> Jones and Smith are discussing which moral principles are undeniable. Robinson hears them, and finds that each seems to follow what the other says. He says their debate is a moral one, but the debaters themselves insist it is a mixture of prudence and epistemology (cp Simons 1976, Watt 1975).

The division of language and life into 'autonomous' areas is logically related to the sets of principles relied on in those areas. So in a dispute about principles an apeal to the division into areas may well be circular - though it may carry conviction with those who agree with us that we have won (cp Palmer *Analogy* 116f).

*   *   *   *

In each of these examples of 'descriptive metaphysics' the inference is p-circular. An argument back to a presupposition cannot provide a proof of it, but only remind us what we are committed to by the concepts we employ.

Regarding the examples presented in these two chapters we have tried to demonstrate only that they are examples of backward argument. Where that leaves the topics in question, would need much further and more expert consideration. It may even turn out that one or two of them do not really proceed 'backwards' in our sense. But if even some of these slogans and theories are accepted as genuine examples, then the transcendental fallacy which earlier chapters laboured to expose is not just a sad bad chapter from philosophy's complicated past, but is very much alive and well.

Chapter Ten

ARGUING TRANSCENDENTALLY

The new line of reasoning tried out by Descartes and by Kant was meant to rebut sceptical querying of our everyday acquaintance with things and people, connections, influence and processes. Certain very basic statements, they claimed, could not be denied without inconsistency. We found that this line of argument cannot be advanced in proof without circularity; but that it could show some people what they already stood committed to.

Having studied several instances of this sort of argument, we should now attempt some generalized account, in the hope that lessons can be learnt from these old and famous fallacies and applied to future, novel instances.

The arguments in question already have a common and accepted name, portentous, awkward to spell, and seemingly mysterious, but too familiar now for any change to be acceptable. We shall first explain what Kant intended by that name: then retail comments made by Kant and others on this sort of argument: and finally venture on our own definition and critique.

As this chapter will summarize our findings about transcendental argument, some degree of repetition is unavoidable.

45. WHAT 'TRANSCENDENTAL' MEANT FOR KANT

Suppose Smith is aware of certain facts. He then sets about 'establishing', in some public and objective way, that he really does have knowledge of those facts: for example, he might construct a

X.45 What 'transcendental' meant for Kant

'proof' of them, and offer it to Brown and Robinson. Now suppose many such efforts are put together and presented as a system, for all to learn and understand, and suppose this leads to the discovery and integration of still further facts. A progressive, co-operative undertaking of this sort is called a 'science'.

Now Jones may enquire what sciences the Smiths and Browns and Robinsons have built so far; and may wonder why it is that they succeeded in constructing just those sciences; and may speculate what other realms of fact might some day be conquered for humanity. These enquiries of Jones are nowadays called 'theory of knowledge' or 'epistemology'. Kant called them 'critical philosophy'.

Our knowledge of facts, in Kant's view, is picked up from day to day in personal experience, but it also contains some elements contributed by us 'in advance' so to speak, of actual experience. How then are those advance-elements acquired? Ought we to rely on them? And how could such a contribution from our side make for knowledge, rather than fiction and fantasy? To these questions and his answers Kant gave a new and special name, 'transcendental'.

Kant explains his own usage of this term, and largely sticks to it:

(1) Knowing this or that is one thing, knowing how those objects can be known is something different, and 'transcendental'(B 25): especially knowing what contribution advance-elements may make to our knowing things.

(2) If some concept, e.g. Space, is so explained as to show how further theorems could derive from it, this exposition is 'transcendental'(B 40).

(3) While many concepts, e.g. 'mountain','dog', are picked up on particular occasions of our individual lives, and are fully justified by those experiences which they help us to absorb and to describe, for some other concepts, e.g. 'cause', no such empirical derivation or 'deduction' is or can ever be available. But we may still try to show by argument how thay can properly apply to particular items of our lived experience (B 116,125). Such a 'transcendental deduction' will "make knowledge

X.45 What 'transcendental' meant for Kant

possible" by showing how such concepts, although not abstracted from experience, can however be used in mastering and digesting that experience (cp Crawford 1962, Aquila 1976).

'Transcendental' thus means for Kant 'making knowledge possible (especially non-empirical)'.

Some account of where Kant got the term is given below (Note E to #49).

46. KANT'S REMARKS ON TRANSCENDENTAL PROOF

In the second edition of the Critique Kant offered a 'transcendental exposition' of Space and Time, to explain how and why perception involves these as advance-elements. Such an 'exposition', he remarks, must show

(1) that the knowledge we do have does derive from the concepts in question, provided

(2) these are understood as advance-elements (B 40).

These requirements simply summarize the backward argument from science (cp # 22 above).

Physics, like geometry, can be a science only if its objects are to some extent home-made. But judgments like 'the fire makes the kettle boil' also involve advance-elements, as perceptions did. The exposition of these contributions will show how we could have a science of the world. The application of these 'categories' however seems to Kant to need further justification, which he offers in a 'transcendental deduction'. This is compared to a lawyer's chain of authorities exhibiting a 'right', i.e. a basis for complaint or claim. For the categories, this right will be established by an abstract argument, showing how concepts not obtained through experience can still properly apply within experience (B 117; cp Genova 1982).

An empirical 'deduction' would proceed by exhibiting the object from which the concept was derived: produce a dog, and that justifies your saying "dog". A transcendental deduction works the other way: here "the concept makes the object possible" (B 125): and the argument must demonstrate how this is done, i.e. show that our world of things

X.46 Kant's remarks on transcendental proof

is made by our applying the categories to our disorganized experience; and that we could not get to 'things' in any other way. Such a 'deduction' justifies advance-concepts by their results, pragmatically: though Kant repeatedly slips back into phrases suggestive of some positive onward-moving 'proof'.

This epistemological enquiry or 'transcendental philosophy' is set out as a system. It is of course helpful to have our items of advance-knowledge all displayed in neat order. Unfortunately the only neat arrangement thought presentable by Kant - and perhaps by his readers - is the deductive structure of geometry. Kant's findings are in consequence set out as a new and non-empirical science, complete with theorems 'proved' by News-from-Nowhere principles.

Kant sometimes writes as though the theory of knowledge were his own discovery. He did work out a new approach to the topic, in a thorough-going and systematic way. We can hardly expect him also to provide a full critical analysis of his own new line of argument. But he does offer some comments on this, in the Doctrine of Method, suggesting three maxims to help avoid asking the impossible (B 814f).

Rule I. Before trying to prove any advance-proposition, see if appropriate materials are available, as premisses (e.g. do not try to prove the Causal Law from abstract ideas alone).

Rule II. For each advance-proposition there can be only one proof, e.g. Universal Causality is provable only by analysing what counts as an 'event'.

Rule III. The proof must be positive, not indirect ("ostensive not apagogic"), i.e must not proceed by disproving the contrary: thus a proof that God's non-existence is inconceivable might only reflect our intellectual feebleness. There is however a certain indirectness in a transcendental proof, for the informative advance-theorems which serve as principles in that system are not themselves deduced from any higher principle; indeed, how could they be, while remaining principles? They are established by a sideways reference to 'possible experience': e.g. every event must have a cause, since otherwise we could neither recognise nor connect 'events'. The proof of the principle thus

X.46 Kant's remarks on transcendental proof

lies in the experience it renders possible, which therefore 'presupposes' it B 765).

These rules and remarks bring out certain features found in transcendental arguments (Kant does not use that precise phrase, but "proof of a transcendental principle" comes to much the same). The argument starts from some theorem or concept, C, already in regular and recognized employment in daily life and in the world of science: something so fundamental and so well established that seriously doubting it would be ridiculous. This item of basic intellectual equipment is then analysed and found to presuppose a certain principle, P, and that principle is then asserted as true, because presupposed by C.

On this account, Rule I means that you should set about proving 'transcendentally' only those principles which indubitable or unavoidable theorems or concepts presuppose. Rule II claims that each principle has only one such proof; perhaps because the process of proof involves internal analysis of that principle, and anything which takes to bits must have just one set of bits. Rule III requires that the principle be positively presupposed: it is not enough that its contrary would be in̲sufficient to 'render knowledge possible'. The remark that proof works 'sideways' corresponds to our name 'backward argument': the principle is not to be derived from some higher and more general statement, but demonstrated as unavoidably required for our knowledge of something we already claim to know.

According to Rule II, an advance-principle like 'every event has a cause' can be proved in only one way: by analysing 'event' to show that such could be known to us only if that principle does hold. The proof proceeds from the presupposition(s) of the concept 'event'; each such concept has only the presupposition(s) that it has; so no other proof along those lines is possible. There is however no reason why a presupposition P of concept C should not also be ingredient in concept D: so a similar line of proof might be offered for two quite different principles.

*   *   *   *

X.46 Kant's remarks on transcendental proof

Kant's 'rules' do not offer a systematic account of transcendental reasoning, only some pertinent remarks; but these do serve to show what sort of arguments he had in mind. We must now ask if this group forms a definite, distinct and novel 'sort', a specific and individual mode of reasoning.

47. WHAT ARE TRANSCENDENTAL ARGUMENTS?

The name 'transcendental' is to select a certain group of arguments for further scrutiny. Each scholar is of course theoretically free to select any group he likes, but in practice he will hold and help his readers only if his usage is more or less continuous with Kant's. It is also important that the proposed grouping really forms a class, so that study of some members can lead us to reasoned predictions about other members of the group. This latter 'inductive' requirement is more difficult to satisfy.

Arguments can be grouped by the conclusions they support, by the premisses from which they start, or by the route taken to the conclusion from the premisses; or in several of these ways (cp Davis 1978, Gram 1978).

(1) Transcendental conclusions. Kant's remarks were directed to proofs of transcendental 'principles'. These principles are informative and non-empirical; and are supposed to explain how it is that our knowledge of things can include (other) informative and yet non-empirical elements. So the proof must show the possibility of arriving synthetically and a priori at some knowledge of things which was not contained in the concept of them (B 811: cp Cramer 1977). As these principles demonstrate how knowledge is after all possible, we may call them 'anti-sceptical'.

Kant has his own theory of how humans get acquainted with their world. Not surprisingly, his principles show how knowledge is possible on that theory (cp Kalin 1977, Benton 18). But his way of establishing these principles may still help others who, preferring some other theory-of-knowledge, espouse other transcendental principles to vindicate that knowledge against sceptical attack.

X.47 What _are_ transcendental arguments?

(2) Transcendental premisses. The conclusion that knowledge is indeed possible for us will require epistemic premisses (Gram 1971). And Kant does start from items or systems of knowledge taken to be irrefutable, just as Descartes starts from a single item, known indefeasibly. In their texts, of course, we find 'I think' and 'There are things', but these are to be read with a perpetual rubric: We know beyond peradventure that I think, etc.

Parallel to this 'I think' we can devise a whole series of incontrovertibles, remarks which defeat denial by providing an instance of what would be denied: 'I am talking', 'this sentence is in English', 'graffiti catch the eye, O.K.?' (cp Meynell 1980, and above #14). Cogito-type arguments can be founded on any 'privileged' propositions of this sort.

Kant first sets out from some given positive science, e.g. geometry. Later he argues from a type of discourse, e.g. talk about real ongoing Things. This more comprehensive starting-point is harder to reject, though it may result in conclusions which are that much emptier. But it does increase the range of application of transcendental arguments.

Whatever the starting-point, some prior reasoning may be needed in favour of accepting it. In the case of privileged propositions like 'I think', we can proceed by showing the contradiction implicit in denying them, as in an ad absurdum argument. This preliminary inference is thus indirect in form. But the main transcendental proof is not indirect. It runs forward, not back from denying a contradiction or a falsity (Genova 1980, cp Gram 177f).

A transcendental argument must start out from some knowledge-claim. Does the reader accept it? - that is the real point. A sceptic will not, of course; he would hardly be a sceptic if he did. But he may find he has already conceded it, in his reasoned profession of a sceptic's faith. Perhaps the real force of transcendental persuasion lies not in conjuring unwelcome conclusions out of harmless-looking premisses, but in getting would-be sceptics to see that _they_ are in no position to deny those premisses (cp Strawson Individuals 106).

X.47 What _are_ transcendental arguments?

(3) **Transcendental reasoning.** Does the conclusion follow by some ordinary principle of inference, in a transcendental argument? Or is its connection with the premisses peculiar and 'non-analytic'? This is not to suggest that all such arguments are equally reliable; but that they should not all be rejected en masse for failing unsuitably rigorous standards of validity (cp Körner 1977). A good transcendental argument, on this view, is not a bad deductive one, but a good persuasion of some other sort, whose standards have yet to be worked out. Much the same has been said about inductive arguments, and could also be said about those from analogy or even from authority (cp Strawson Theory 233, Wilkerson 1970).

The special relationship on which transcendental arguments are supposed to turn is a special condition sufficient and supposedly unique; as for example in Kant's Refutation of Idealism:

> A sequence of experiences could, we presume, be taken by somebody as 'his' only if he saw himself as distinct from 'other' things. But we have some such experience, so besides us there must be some 'external' things (B 274, cp Wilkerson 203).

Necessary conditions are of course familiar. The 'only' is harder to handle. It says that no other sufficient condition (for the knowledge, experience or what-have-you) is conceivable (by us). Clearly we cannot say what others may or may not manage one day to conceive. It is not even clear how we can make out from 'within' the limits to our own imaginative and constructive intellectual powers.

There is certainly a puzzle here, though not a very novel one. But does that puzzle reside in the actual reasoning involved, or in the premisses from which it starts? The answer to this is partly up to us, as a more familiar 'unusual' type of argument may show:

> That man has a helmet on
> So he's probably a policeman.

This inference, we say, is not deductive but 'statistical', for while most helmets are on policemen's heads, some are on firemen's, and a few on those of dramatic romantics re-'fighting' Great

X.47 What *are* transcendental arguments?

Battles of Our Past. Now these alternatives can all be summed up in an extra premiss:

> As 80% of helmets are worn by policemen, any given helmet-wearer has a 4:1 chance of being a policeman

The remaining reasoning is then deductive and unremarkable:

> This man is wearing a helmet
> So 4 to 1 he's a policeman.

This inference can now be appraised by the usual deductive standards, leaving all the 'unusual' aspect in that extra and apparently factual premiss, where we have some chance of seeing what to do with it.

Re-cast in this way Kant's Refutation reads

1. Where we can see one way in which something that does happen could happen, and can't see any other way, we must suppose it to happen in that way.

2. The only way we can see for a self to integrate and appropriate its serial experiences is by regarding itself as distinct from other things.

3. But we do so integrate our serial experiences.

So 4. We must suppose ourselves distinct from 'external' things.

The structure of this argument is unremarkable. Whether those premisses are all true or could be known by us, will be considered in the next section.

Most transcendental arguments are 'regressive' in character. Some knowledge or experience is taken as given first, other items required as preconditions for such experience or knowledge are then explored; these items are then alleged to be available, for behold, those things were *given*, to which these items are pre-requisite (Ameriks 1978). This parallels the argument 'back' from a presupposing reference to the item presupposed; and resembles the line of reasoning Kant called 'analytic' (Baum 1977; cp above #16, #23).

X.47 What are transcendental arguments?

Regressive arguments do not however involve any special sort of inference, but run parallel to causal arguments and to many other reasonings from 'only-if'. Given that thunder is caused only by lightning, i.e. (at least) that thunder can happen only if lightning happens first, then from a heard thunder-clap we can reason regressively to some previous lightning which, perhaps, we did not see. This argument simply affirms the antecedent, a valid mood for any only-if. How we could know, that only lightning causes thunder, is a fascinating but a further point, and concerns the major premiss, not the line of argument. Neither causal arguments, nor regressive arguments in general are special or peculiar as arguments.

The precise direction of Kant's 'Transcendental Deduction' is a matter of dispute (see above # 25f). It does take Experience for granted: we think we live with Things and work on them and they on us. It alleges that we construct those Things from bits and pieces, from muddles and mixtures and sequences of sensed-qualities. It concludes that connecting-Things-up causally (etc) is all right because it was by connecting that we constructed Things (and Us).

The argument that its all right for you to take it out because you put it in (B 125,159) is not regressive in character. It relies on a traditional and perhaps picturesque idea, that our own ideas are fully known by us and us alone (see above #20). The main effort goes into showing that Things are really made by us. It then follows, by a 'forward' argument, that we, the constructors, can have a science of our Things.

The Deduction is transcendental in Kant's sense: it shows how knowledge can be had by men. However, if we decide to restrict our term 'transcendental argument' to regressive ones then the Deduction (as just expounded) is not one of them. That may seem an unfortunate result. But all Kant's other major arguments in the Critique (Aesthetic, Analogies, Refutation of Idealism) are regressive. And Kant introduces the term 'deduction' because he felt it differed from a proof (cp Benton 1978).

X.47 What are transcendental arguments?

    A transcendental argument, then, is anti-sceptical: it aims to establish something needed for human knowledge and which sceptics say is unreliable or not available. The argument starts from 'epistemic' premisses. One of these describes conditions alleged necessary for our referring properly to X, correctly using concept (or 'discourse') Y, or claiming knowledge Z. The other premiss alleges that reference X, concept or discourse Y or knowledge Z is O.K., in working order or available. The logical step to that conclusion from those premisses, in a well-formed transcendental argument, is short, simple, familiar and quite reliable. The only question, then, is whether those premisses really are available to us, in the precise form required (cp Leaman 1980).

48. ASSESSING TRANSCENDENTAL PREMISSES

Premiss One: that S presupposes P. This is made out, we said, 'by inspection' of S and P, i.e. by noticing that P is in a special way ingredient in S, so that S would be improper in some way if P were not available for thought and reference.

    This account takes very much for granted the language or conceptual scheme within which S, supposedly, presupposes P. We all do take our language and concepts for granted, for only so can we use them to construct or exchange thoughts about things. The Boy Scout learning Morse may well wish Mr Morse had been a bit more regular, one dot for A, two for B and so on: and no doubt alternative codes could be constructed from the same materials, and some such might even be superior to Morse. But it is better not to raise this point with the wireless operator when the ship is foundering. No, indeed, not then. Still the mere possibility of such alternatives does mean that any transcendental truths discovered about Morse, e.g. that the simplest strongest letters come in TOM, are just truths about Morse, known true of and about that code alone.

X.48 Assessing transcendental premisses

By the same token, categorial discoveries made by the aid of our language or conceptual scheme may be, for all we know, no more than that. For consider what would be required to prove the contrary:

> To think is, to differentiate. To draw distinctions, we need some basic common features and some discriminating attributes; and there may, for all we know, be several sets on the market, requiring the customer to 'choose'. Faced with this possibility, we try to construct an argument to show that in a given area there was only one set of basic attributes available for use. Now we might indeed show, working from 'inside', so to speak, that one such 'categorial scheme' is in fact available, namely ours, but there can be no basis for a claim that this scheme is unique (Körner 1966a).

The proper task of a transcendental deduction, on this view, is to take one set of basic concepts or categories actually in use, and show just how they work (Körner 1967, Rorty 1977).

Now this critique clearly starts from the sort of <u>premisses</u> available for transcendental inference: you can say that some concepts are in use but you can't hope to show that no others could be used instead - though of course we may claim that <u>we can't see</u> what others could be used.

At this point Kant's Transcendental Idealism offers an interesting parallel. He claimed to have shown that Space and Time are our only ways to organize phenomena, which explained why all our phenomena were in fact so organized. In this claim he went too far; at most he had shown that Space and Time might be just our ways of ordering phenomena, that for all we know these might be formative structures which we impose upon our world. This more modest claim would leave open the possibility that, for all we know, Space and Time are real after all: that the world just happens to be constructed along the lines that we have taken to organizing it. But possibilities are only possibilities. If the question is: What do we know about the Universe? then on either version the reply must be that Space and Time are <u>not known</u> to be ultimately real (cp Palmer <u>Logic</u> 53, 174).

X.48 Assessing transcendental premisses

As far as we can tell, certain 'categories' are basic for all human thought. There is no hope at all of showing any more than that: of proving them unique, so that even God must think with them. So it is unwise to blow them up into General Truths about the Universe. They are species-specific, and may even be culture-bound.

This critique runs parallel to the view of the Cogito as a 'linguistic' argument (above, #17). However, as 'our language' includes in effect all others which translate intelligibly for us, and 'our culture' takes in its sweep those of all peoples elsewhere or at other times of whose activities and statements we can make any sort of sense, this restriction is surely none too rigorous. We can afford to be culture-bound to this extent, since all our conceivable knowledge, data or interests lie within this circle of our fairyland.

So much for the range of presuppositional discoveries. We must also ask what status they enjoy. What sort or grade of truth is contained in the statement that S presupposes P? And how may we discover it?

In practice we come across such facts by 'just thinking', i.e. by reflection on the structure of our concepts and the proprieties of conversation. We do not organize observations or perform experiments, for concepts and proprieties do not lie outside of us to be observed or experimented on.

Even on this isolationist view of conceptual and linguistic skills, it does not follow that such truths are known a priori or with greater certainty: only that they are not acquired experimentally. They may still be empirical, items picked up as life goes on by observing them; only the object of our observations is ourselves, our habits and preferences and inconceivabilities. And self-observation is not always treated as reliable.

Some will deny that this isolationist account could possibly be right. Terms and concepts, they say, are units or embodiments of skills, and skills are gained in interplay in an already formulated game. We do not need to look 'inside' ourselves to discover the structure of a sentence or a term; but should study instead the conventions of our Society, for it was by internalizing those conventions that

X.48 Assessing transcendental premisses

we also joined the game. Now conventions are open to objective study, even to experiment, though they cannot be weighed or exhibited or passed around. And the knowledge gained by such study is of necessity empirical (Chisholm 1978).

This does not make transcendental reasoning less certain than that practised in the other natural sciences, but it does undermine its claim to be _more_ certain or basic or reliable. Theories about a priori knowledge are not for that reason known a priori, any more than a book about crime is for that reason criminal. 'Transcendental' theories are indeed prior to the sciences they describe and seek to justify: prior in the logical sense, though in fact developed only afterwards. But that does not make them more-than-scientific, or specially dependable.

This point is sometimes glimpsed by Kant, but never fully grasped. He usually writes as if his Critique should provide a general super-science to which departmental sciences could then resort for a supply of principles: a Central Veracity Generating Board distributing Truth and Light by a Notional Grid through all the commonwealth of science. But his Critique is not above or before the special sciences. It runs alongside, like the rescue phone-line on the motorway. Where the critique gets its own information from is a quite separate question to be considered on its own (Nelson II 168f, expounding Fries).

Premiss Two: that S is proper, genuine, available. A transcendental argument starts from 'epistemic' premisses, i.e. from statements about human knowledge; one of which lays down conditions for some such knowledge to occur, while the other states that it really does occur. Does this second premiss beg the question which the argument was intended to resolve?

In every valid argument the conclusion contains information already presented in the premisses; no more, and no different. It may be objected that such arguments are not informative, as the conclusion only re-presents what was already given in the premisses. Another critic will reject as question-begging any argument in which the conclusion reached <u>was</u> already given in the

X.48 Assessing transcendental premisses

premisses. Both complainants are crying for the moon. An argument can only be developed from what is given. To venture beyond that given may well seem more interesting and informative, but it will infallibly be unreliable. The only novelty permitted in deductive reasoning is that of combination and re-arrangement: the conclusion may bring out something which the premisses do jointly indicate but which was not actually stated in either on its own.

The complaint of question-begging is only in place where <u>one</u> premiss contains all the controversial matter that the conclusion requires: where the arguer need not 'put two and two together' but only take the wrappings off (Palmer 1981b). Transcendental arguments are not especially liable to this particular fault. But they do all suffer from a closely related fallacy.

In an argument from presupposition the second term, P, is ingredient in the main term, S. This means that S cannot be confirmed without first making sure of P: after which, argument back from S to the truth of P is quite superfluous. For this reason all such 'backward' inference is bound to be p-circular (see above #11). And all transcendental arguments are backward arguments, for they all start from some statement or science or communication-system as <u>given</u> in good working order, and work back from it to the conditions it is alleged to presuppose.

Such presumptive circularity is endemic in all transcendental reasoning. This feature is due to the relation and arrangement of the terms: the first premiss not only makes P a necessary condition for the availability of S, but also makes it an ingredient <u>in</u> S, so that it is pointless to argue back again from S to P. Those who have called such argument question-begging have perhaps been noting this feature, but mis-naming it.

In the <u>Cogito</u> the minor premiss 'I do think' turned out to <u>include</u> all other starting-points: for if I assert that I walk or I talk or I nod or I blink these claims are all open to doubt, whereas 'I think that I blink' remains unshakable. For this excellent reason Descartes regarded 'I think' as the best and most basic starting-point available to anyone.

151

X.48 Assessing transcendental premisses

In a similar way Kant's starting-points of Newtonian physics and Euclidean geometry can be extended to entire subject-areas. Perhaps we should take Pythagoras' theorem as in some way revisable, but still the revised version will also be geometrical in character. So there is still some geometry: and the geometry-there-still-is (in the last analysis) can serve to start our transcendental arguments.

Kant's exposition, on this view, suffers from too much reliance on Euclid and Newton, whose systems now seem less definitive than he supposed; but the general line of argument is safe, and we can still be sure of what the geometry of the Last Day will be found to presuppose. We may not be sure what that is, just yet, but we still stand committed, come what may, to whatever it may turn out to be.

The view that all our theories are in principle revisable seems both radical and safe: safe against upset by future revisions, anyway. But it can hardly be used to re-inforce transcendental argument; for we do not yet know what we do not yet know, nor can we make out what it will presuppose.

A further generalizing step has been taken, to make the second premiss more impregnable. Instead of arguing from particular known sciences, or from the Science that they one day may become, a start is made from the 'field of discourse' in which discussion of such sciences would move:

> Your morality may be different from mine. Maybe neither of us can be sure of establishing any one moral judgment as incontrovertible. Still, the fact that we go on discussing them shows our continued allegiance to certain principles of rational debate which are really moral in character. No party to a moral discussion, then, can be allowed to reject these moral principles.

Comment on this widening of the argument was offered earlier (#44). Our present point is simply that premiss Two is made wider and wider so as to be less deniable, but that each widening must also be an emptying. An inference whose premisses no-one will deny may demonstrate things that no-one would bother to assert.

X.48 Assessing transcendental premisses

Missing premisses. It may be said that the premisses put forward in a transcendental argument do not on their own enforce the conclusion there alleged: that an extra premiss would be needed to complete the argument. In particular, it has been alleged that all transcendental arguments secretly rely on some version of the Verification Principle; so if that is not available for use, transcendental conclusions can never be soundly reached. But if that Principle were available, on the open market, we would hardly waste time on the detour of transcendental inference (Stroud 1968, Hacker 1972).

In the major premiss it is alleged that some knowledge, experience or statement S presupposes P, i.e. S would be out of place or impossible or not available to us unless P were there. Would it not be enough, the sceptic asks, if everyone believed that P? For example, suppose real extended solid Things were taken by simply everyone as part of the furniture of earth. This question is a tricky one. Answer Yes, and the sceptic will say that your argument only re-confirms that this and that are generally believed; which the sceptic also admits, for that was where he started from. "But it's only a belief" he sceptically says, "you can't ever show that it is true". Answer No, and the sceptic will ask you to show what difference it makes, for the purpose of people saying, practising or knowing S, that they should know P to be true, and not just believe it so.

It is at this point that appeal to the Verification Principle might unwarily be made. The principle claims that what you mean by a statement depends on what you know. If this principle is available for use, you can answer No to the Sceptic, for the Principle will confirm that knowledge of P is indeed required, that universal unquestioning belief will not be good enough.

According to this complaint, the anti-sceptical conclusion of the argument would follow from the premiss 'S could not occur, were it not for the truth of P'; but the premiss actually available is only 'S could not occur, did not everyone believe that P'. The arguer is challenged to supply the difference.

X.48 Assessing transcendental premisses

By way of encouragement the complainant then remarks that he could always use a Verification Principle to stuff the hole, but anyone equipped with one of those will hardly need a transcendental argument.

To work a transcendental argument we must first know that S presupposes P, i.e. that S would be improper unless P were true. Stroud says we can only detect impropriety in S due to P not being generally believed. So his suggestion of a missing premiss boils down to the claim that the major premiss as stated cannot be known by us (cp Tlumak 1976, Rosenberg 1975).

All these critiques thus reduce to simple and familiar advice: don't accept a conclusion unless you are quite sure about its premisses.

*   *   *   *

The major premiss of a tanscendental argument states a logical or conceptual priority: that S has P as an ingredient. Such statements are often made with great confidence and without much scientific ceremony, because we are extremely familiar with the structure of the language we use all day and every day. If disputed, such statements could be confirmed only by empirical language-study.

To that extent this premiss is 'linguistic' and therefore culture-bound. Even if we found that in every known language or culture, S (or its equivalent) presupposes P (or its equivalent), we could never prove this to be a unique and necessary relation of ingredience. That S presupposes P, is a factual remark.

In the minor premiss some knowledge or usage S is alleged to be 'all right'. That may well be so. And in the business of living it may be all right for us to proceed on the basis that it is so. But it cannot be right for us to employ such an item in a proof of P, for P (being ingredient in S) would have to be checked first, in the process of confirming S.

This point cannot be evaded by making this premiss still more general. That talk does happen, is probably harder to deny, than that Euclidean geometry is final and definitive. But it is also harder to see what talk as talk must presuppose.

X.48 Assessing transcendental premisses

It is also said that arguing transcendentally assumes a further unstated premiss, more or less the same as the Verification Principle. That is not quite correct, but may serve as a way to present a fork: are you proving knowledge from what we already know, or pretending it because of what everybody must believe?

Although such argument cannot prove, from S, that P, it is in place as reminding us that we are presupposing P - and so had better not go denying it. The argument is good ad hominem, i.e for refuting some extreme statements by one who already accepts these premisses (Griffiths 1969).

The bandying of such arguments may well tend to increase the national output of remarks such as 'S presupposes P', some of which are true and may be somehow verified. It is probably good for us to realise our conceptual priorities, to map out the linguistic web around which we so nimbly crawl. In that indirect way, transcendental arguments are good for spiders like ourselves.

49. CONCLUDING CHALLENGE ON TRANSCENDENTAL PROOF

The fallacy called p-circularity is involved in all argument 'back' to a presupposition, since that presupposition would itself need to be verified, in arriving at the premisses. Now, do we claim that all transcendental arguments move 'backward' in this unfortunate sense?

We do claim that the Cogito of Descartes, the central reasoning of Kant's first Critique, and several modern examples discussed in the last chapter (#44) are all transcendental arguments and do all run backward in this ineffective way.

To show that all transcendental arguments whatever do so run, we should need an agreed definition of a 'transcendental argument'. But this is a term of art whose precise definition is hotly disputed among practitioners, and which is not used by anybody else. In this situation, an evaluation of such arguments based on a definition will make that definition evaluative in effect, thus ensuring the continuance of definitional debate, and probably casting further darkness on the point really at issue.

X.49 Concluding challenge on transcendental proof

To avoid this, we propose a challenge. If anyone wishes to put forward what he calls a transcendental argument, let him show that the premisses are really available to him when the conclusion is not. If all transcendental arguers can do that, then they have gained their point, and it would be merely cantankerous for us to go on disputing terminology. If any cannot, then that is where his particular problem lies. He needs to make his own argument work properly, not to prove in some general way that "it ought to work".

Note E. Why 'transcendental'? Transcend means 'go beyond'. The transcendent is something right outside our ordinary range, far above (or below) all the separate seems-to-me's of everyday experience.
Transcendental, in Kant, means 'making knowledge possible', especially the bits contributed, he thinks, by us. No-one now knows how Kant arrived at this new meaning for the term. That leaves us free to speculate:

(1) Descriptive terms vary very much in range: thus 'jagged' applies only to edges of some hard material, while 'tall' can describe people, buildings and stories, and 'rich' suits people, countries, decoration, cake and stew. Going even further we find a short list of absolutely basic predicates which apply completely generally. Anything and everything can be said to Be, One, True and Good. These fundamental features of the creation, which transcend all minor divisions and home-made categories, were called 'transcendentals' in the mediaeval philosophy which still formed part of the curriculum when Kant went to university.
(2) Among Kant's immediate predecessors in Germany, certain theories, e.g. in cosmology, could be called transcendental as being completely general and so presumably not learnt from particular experience but somehow given-in-advance. And one writer spoke of the several properties of salt or steel as being "one transcendentally", meaning that each substance has some central essence which lies behind and explains its surface properties. The earlier meaning 'basic and completely general' here branches out to include the notions 'explaining' and 'given-in-advance' (Angelelli 1972, Hinske 35).
(3) Kant's own system starts out from the suggestion that Space and Time, although genuine features of our lived experience, are 'transcendentally ideal', that is, subjective, in the last analysis. Now whatever there really is, in the last analysis and before we mess it up by knowing it, is presumably responsible for those joint productions that he calls phenomena, which we can have knowledge of. Thus what transcends our little world is also responsible for it, and makes our knowledge of it possible.

It would be nice to know if this is how Kant came to use 'transcendental' to mean 'making knowledge possible'. But we don't know. This is just one guess.

Chapter Eleven

CHANGING SPECTACLES

Transcendental arguments are supposed to show scepticism false, on the ground that, if it were true, the point could not even be discussed. This line of backward reasoning is always p-circular, and so incompetent as proof. But it can serve as a warning to persons holding certain views, that scepticism had better not be professed by them, if they still have any fear of inconsistency.

How stands the case with human knowledge, then, if these limits on transcendental argumentation prove quite general? A full answer might require another book, or two; here we shall only sketch the main alternatives.

50. BACK TO SQUARE ONE

Refuting an argument does not change anything, except the relative position of the arguers. It undoes whatever the argument was meant to do. All the options are open once again.

The argument just refuted, in earlier chapters, was anti-sceptical. This suggests that Scepticism stands as one of the options, once again, until or unless refuted by some other argument or evidence. Not that this tells in its favour, at all; it is just that one of its intending executioners has been retired.

If 'Scepticism' were the name of a genuine alternative, one of several consistent and systematic schemes of thought which thinkers have to choose between, then indeed it would 'stand' again, once transcendental reasoning had been put aside.

XI.50 Back to Square One

But 'scepticism' is not the name of a genuine theory or systematic scheme of thought. Real sceptics are very hard to find, just because it is not a genuine alternative theory. It is a mode of presentation for a topic in the theory of knowledge; a mode strictly misleading though pleasingly dramatic. That topic is: What ultimate backing have we, for what we claim to know? (cp above #6). So the real question is: what bearing would successful transcendental arguments have had on that topic? And what difference must their inevitable failure make?

A successful argument would 'justify' the principles and/or concepts of some present science, in a way felt appropriate and found comforting. That is, it would show why those principles and concepts can be used in making sense of our experience: that such application is proper, scientific and respectable.

Now, failing such justification, what alternatives remain for us to face?

(1) If one line of justifying argument should fail, perhaps some kind person will replace it with a better line of argument.
(2) If not, then our non-empirical concepts and principles will remain unjustified, and so cannot be used. Science will close down.
(3) Or perhaps we shall carry on just the same, even though they are unjustified; just remarking over our shoulders that science, after all, does work.
(4) Or we may deny that the 'question of justification' makes any sort of sense.

Whether (1) some better line of argument can be devised, to replace transcendental inference, is a question for posterity. There are no other candidates at present, but no-one can say what the future holds in store. We can however flag the pitfalls on the way, and indicate what sort and strength of premiss would be required for such a 'super-transcendental argument' (Govier 1978). That done, some interim professional gloom seems sensible.

XI.50 Back to Square One

Option 2 is to close down Science. But of course Science is not going to close down just because some professors of philosophy cannot satisfy themselves of its intellectual respectability. This is not just because science is profitable, or even indispensable, nor because scientists and their followers are dogmatic and insensitive, but because their discoveries are thought more reliable than any philosophers' queries as to whether such discoveries are possible. Every query presupposes a theory, and the theory on which their queries rest is itself open to considerable doubt.

The fact that 'they won't close it down' is frankly faced in option 3, and made into a principle: Science works, so its concepts and structures are bound to be alright. Opponents of this view concede that the success of science is incontrovertible, but they still object to making a virtue out of that necessity. They reject the pragmatic <u>inference</u>.

The fourth option seems different and sounds more radical. Knowledge has no foundations, and requires none. It is silly to worry about not finding them, indeed it was silly to go and look for them. 'Justification' is a non-event. Theoretical theory-of-knowledge is a waste of time (Bernsen 25, Rorty 1977, Stiffler 1984).

Scepticism (so-called) consists of professing not to know something that someone thinks you ought to know. If Smith regards weather-forecasting as an expensive guess, Brown will call Smith a sceptic only if Brown thinks there is more to it than that. For this reason, non-believers in Santa Claus are accounted sceptics only in the nursery. On the first three options, then, we feel ourselves 'sceptics' for not having provided that justification that science does require; but on option 4 we reject that requirement, and so can renounce justification without feeling that we are sceptics for having failed. We didn't find Atlantis, but then, it wasn't there.

Only options 3 and 4 are open to us now. The pragmatist (3) says "Accept the science of geometry - for what it's worth": which seems very close to saying "geometry is a science - just look at it - so it has to be alright": which is what the transcendental persuasions come to in the end.

The slogan 'Don't ask for foundations' (4) does not mean that all our sciences are built on sand. Each has its own foundations, and a well-built one still differs from a shack. But there is no general metaphysical science of epistemological foundations, underpinning all of them. Theory-of-knowledge is just another science or discipline, with no special rights or virtues. It is not prior to the rest of them.

The aim of this broadside, presumably, is just to make science safe for pragmatists.

Only one distinct option remains open to us, then: that systems cannot be judged externally by what they are built on, or with, but only by what they are and do for us.

True enough; but there are still some questions to be asked about their 'principles': how we come by them, and whether there are several sets of them that we shall have to choose between.

51. JUSTIFYING PRINCIPLES

Every system of thought requires principles. A deductive system requires axioms, statements taken as true to start with, and from which all the other statements, the theorems, are proved. Each theorem is supported by a proof from prior theorems, and these are proved from yet earlier ones, but this regress of reasons has to come to an end, or the business of proving could never have begun. the system can't be <u>all</u> theorems. There must be some principles as <u>well</u>, unproved original starting-points. To ask for such principles to be <u>proved</u> is just uneducated; but it is not foolish to ask whether they are acceptable, and why (cp Foster 1935).

Non-deductive systems also require starting-points. The system supports some statements by (non-deductive) reasoning from other statements, and so on. This giving of non-deductive reasons also has to terminate. The system cannot consist entirely of results.

In addition to starting-points, each system relies on logical principles by which to do the reasoning. These may also be justified by appeal to

XI.51 Justifying principles

more fundamental principles, but there has to be some supreme Court for this sequence of appeals, if any logical principles are to be justified thereby.

Every orderly system of thought or reasoning requires certain principles, some as starting-points for reasoning and some as rules to reason by, if that system is to establish any results by reasoning. This is not an excuse for swallowing just anything that someone puts forward as a principle; of course the results will be no more sensible or reliable than the principles they were shown to follow by or from. But it does remind us that systems can at best only show conclusions _following_. The system points out a way from A to B, and invites us to travel by that way, just supposing we have first arrived at A.

No prior justification, in the sense of proof, can be given for a set of principles; for if it were, then they would be no longer principles. The system would grow backward by that step, whose starting-point would be the system's new and unproved principles. So offers to _prove_ principles can only move the problem one stage further back (cp Nelson II 43, and above #22).

A pragmatic justification works the other way: "Look what a good system we have here, so clear, so convincing, so full of truth, so fertile of discovery! What more could you desire?"

The transcendental justification was meant to run alongside: "But for these constructive principles, you could not make what sense you now do out of sense-experience. Without them, you could not even meet with Things, in the maelstrom of consciousness." This is to show that physicists cannot consistently abjure the categories - and that each of us is a budding physicist (cp Genova 1978).

Either way, we have to decide what are the things we just must claim to know. What are the lynch-pins of science? These may be uncovered by systematic questioning, revealing their true position in the structure of human knowledge. Alternatively, if some characteristic features of such basic, protocol, original items of knowledge were made out, we could go round listing items which do display those characters (Nelson II 181, expounding Fries). Which is just what Descartes

XI.51 Justifying principles

hoped to do, though he planned to start from what we definitely had, and not from what we could not do without.

At this point the no-foundations school appears rather similar. They do not abstain from all justification. They do say, rightly, that not everything can be justified. You can't show that knowledge is knowledge after all, as this statement itself would also require to be known. And where reasons are given, this school correctly remarks that you can't go on for ever giving them; that justification stops when you get down to principles, and you can't hope in the same way to justify the principles.

Do they also say that principles cannot be justified or justifiably preferred in any way at all? That you just have to 'accept our Universe' and that is that? Kant talks like this about his category-list; and we promptly correct him by saying that there are alternatives. Not that we have alternative universes to enjoy, Startrek minibreaks from the familiar weary round. Nor do we have much choice about accepting ours, as regularly understood; but we do know of some alternative ways of making sense of it. And if there are alternative ways then it can't be the case that we have to accept this or that one of them. So we would like to know what we are choosing between, and would value some explicit statement of reasons for our final preference. Which means 'justifying our principles' in some way.

Having made out what principles, logical or material, form the basis for our systems of reasons, we must consider what alternatives there are, and what reasons could be given for preferring one or another set of them. It has however been suggested that some at least of these principles are absolute presuppositions', not consciously supposed and not verifiable either, being neither true nor false. This seems a variant of the no-justification view, but it may repay further study, if only by clarifying our notion of a principle. It was set out in a clear and persuasive form by Collingwood.

163

52. ABSOLUTE PRESUPPOSITIONS

For Collingwood, scientific, purposeful, orderly thinking consists of asking good questions and then finding evidence to answer them. Now in asking a question we always take something for granted, some situation in which that question arises and outside which it could not sensibly be asked. Thus the question 'What time is it?' presumes some common system of time-measurement, and some clocks to measure it. Some questions presuppose statements which answer previous questions, which in their turn presuppose other statements, and so on ...; and this string of previous questions has a determinate order and, presumably, some starting-point. Thus the question 'Have you stopped beating your wife?' presupposes that you have been beating her, which presupposes that you have a wife whom you can beat, etc (Collingwood 23f).

We may or may not think of the statement presupposed, when asking the question which presupposes it. If we do think of it, we may or may not believe it to be true. Whatever we do think about that presupposition, if it is false in fact then our question, based on it, 'will not arise' but will be out of place; we shall have asked a silly question, a non-sense in that context, though in some other context the same words could compose a question which made perfectly good sense.

A complex question has a whole series of presuppositions running back from it. Most of these answer prior questions, which have presuppositions of their own; but we must suppose that the series terminates. The last member will be presupposition-less, or 'absolute'. There being no prior question for it to answer, it can be neither true nor false. It subsists just by being absolutely presupposed, in these later questions from which we journeyed back to it. And these later questioners will feel uncomfortable when we get to it, quite naturally, for they cannot defend it yet cannot allow that it appear dubious. That is why scientists get shirty if asked how they know that everything that happens has a cause (31).

Absolute presuppositions cannot be believed, not being true or false. They can only be supposed, i.e. taken for granted in the process of asking

XI.52 Absolute presuppositions

questions based on them. Nor can we give reasons for adopting this or that one, for if we could the reason would come first. So we cannot choose rationally which ones to absolutely presuppose. In fact, we pick them up from our society by a process of acculturation: we just get used to using them. The set of absolute presuppositions employed in a given society does change, but slowly and unconsciously, to ease the strains created by the system's incomplete consistency (48n, 74f).

Although not subject to choice, the absolute presuppositions of this or that age or system can be laid bare, by considering the questions and answers based on them. These presupposition-sets, ancient or modern, are not subject to assessment as true or false, but we can hope to make out the transitions by which one set gave way to another, thus leading to a novel school of thought. That a certain school of thought worked on presuppositions A, B, C is a statement of historical fact, and may be true or false. But since such facts are discovered and verified by a special sort of logical detective-work, this discovery and assessment is usually left to a special breed of intellectual historians, traditionally called 'philosophers' (49f; summaries in Ketner 4, Donagan 66).

This scheme is open to immediate objection, on several points:

<u>Questions</u> Not every statement is made in answer to a question; though some question could always be devised for any given statement to be an answer to. But this sort of logical stuffing does not increase understanding, it only thickens books. The regress of presuppositions can be explained just as well, without bringing question and answer into it.

<u>Non-propositions</u> If any presupposition has none of its own, it could still be true or false. Without those properties it could not enjoy other logical relationships such as consistency (which Collingwood re-named 'con-supponibility' 66,331).

<u>Justification</u> A statement which lacks presuppositions might still be justified: for a presupposition is not a reason in favour of the statement which presupposes it, but a situation in which it makes sense to look for reasons, pro

XI.52 Absolute presuppositions

and con. A presuppositionless statement is one so simple that no special situation is required, one in which there are no 'prior questions' to be asked.

<u>The first move fallacy</u> The proposed regress of presuppositions need have no first member. In the regress of movers, it is plausible to urge that someone must have made the first move, at least if we assume an initial state of universal rest. But in a regress of analysis the series is taken as given, first; we cannot say it would never have happened if someone hadn't started it.

<u>No complete sequences</u> Collingwood shows us a regress starting up - Have you stopped beating your wife? - and he shows us one running right back to its 'absolute' origin - Why should everything be caused? - but he leaves us to fill in the middle of these sequences. He starts the unravelling, which gives an idea how it must go on, and also provides a reason why it is bound to terminate. He also provides a well-known instance of what such termination could be like. But we have discarded his reason, and so are left with two ends and nothing in between.

It may well be, then, that the regress he begins would quickly terminate in statements quite simple and wholly unremarkable, like 'there are husbands, and wives' and 'there are times and seasons' and 'beating does take place'.

But marriage, you may say, is a complex human institution, crying out for more analysis. And more can be provided, on demand. When the demand dries up, the analysis will terminate. On this view no presuppositions are in themselves final or original, though some are ultimate for us, when we see no point in further questioning (Ketner 21f).

53. INITIAL ITEMS AND BASIC PRINCIPLES

The simple and acceptable statements in which most presuppositional regresses soon terminate are expressed existentially. This does not mean that they can be verified just by looking around. To be sure, you will see husbands if you look around, but you will see them <u>as</u> husbands only if you know what marriage is. This applies even to the most popular

166

XI.53 Initial items and basic principles

candidates for ostensive definition, e.g. 'dog': you can point one out to me, but that will help me to know what a dog is only if I know about 'animals' already, 'four-legged', 'domestic', 'scavenging' ...My thought-system must have a pretty well dog-shaped blank in it, before you can even start on fitting in the instances.

The questions just asked about husbands, wives and dogs can be asked about any concept that we use. By asking such questions, the simple existential statement 'there are dogs' is replaced by a complex assertion with denoting phrase: 'in our society people keep tame domesticated animals for protection, cuddling or company, e.g. members of the species so-and-so'. The items in this statement need not be simpler or more basic than the item 'dog'. The regress of analysis comes to an end not by reaching rock-bottom, but by our having had enough of it.

The referential presuppositions of a statement do form a system, large or small, which terminates in simple existential claims we find acceptable or obvious. If one of these is questioned, it can be confirmed by indicating one of the items in question - "that man on the left is the President of France" - or by setting out just enough of the conceptual system in which such instances are so described - "in some systems of elective government considerable powers are vested for a period in one man". Explanations of this sort do not yield a definitional system, in which all concepts are traced back to a few primitives; for each explanation uses several terms in explaining one. As a programme of conceptual economy, such reduction is too expensive to be feasible. And the real point of such reductions is quite different. They serve to 'locate' terms in a mainly given framework, not to spin the framework out of nothing as the spider spins his web (Palmer 1966).

Systems of thought have other presuppositions too, methodical or conceptual; e.g. 'every event must have a cause'. These basic working principles are not simple, nor are they existentially expressed. Each has presuppositions of its own: e.g. that some necessity is not merely definitional, or that the course of experience is constituted of discrete 'events'. What makes the principle basic is not its lack of presuppositions, nor our lack of

XI.53 Initial items and basic principles

interest in them, but its relation to the thought-system in which it serves as principle. The principle has been used throughout that laborious construction. Alternatives to it can sometimes be conceived, but not adopted without sacrificing everything that system has achieved. Revising the principle means revising almost everything; that is why we regard it as a principle.

It is of course upsetting if someone queries a principle of a system in which we have invested much, especially if we had never previously noticed our own reliance on that principle. So the 'touchiness' of the topic may serve to warn us when a principle is being criticized, or at least when we are 'getting warm', in a way that a helmet may warn us that a policeman is beneath. But we should not define the notion of a principle by reference to such contingent signs.

We shall want to ask how such principles work in or inform the systems built up by their aid, and how far a system is 'determined' by such principles. This should help us to see how new thought-systems grow up, and why people move across from old to new. All such questions had better be asked about complete and separate (sub-)systems first, e.g. Euclidean geometry, so as to leave us room in which to think around them and conceive alternatives. But we may still hope to apply our findings later on to the whole seamless fabric of human thought, invention and discovery; or to the wardrobe our local culture supplies for us to clothe our thoughts.

The process of Inquiry or revision of belief is described by pragmatists like this: each of us has at each moment a certain set of beliefs or stock responses to our world. Now and then a new and uncomfortable perception upsets the even tenor of our reactionary lives: so we fuss around trimming this and that until the pieces all settle down again. Having revised one or more items to accomodate the awkward customer, we now have a new and satisfying fabric of Belief.

If our beliefs are arranged in an ordered, hierarchic system, like geometry, then the revision will be more or less 'fundamental' according to the place in the system which the belief under revision occupies. So while much scientific work is

XI.53 Initial items and basic principles

undisturbing, progressive and piecemeal, 'advancing the frontiers of knowledge' but not moving the capital, there may from time to time be some more central and pervasive change which because of its systematic consequences is aptly compared to a Revolution at the heart of things. Then a new system is generated; a new science grows up beside the old. The new view cannot be 'taken on board' peacefully or gradually, it is too radical for that. So it is resisted for a time; efforts are redoubled to make the good old systems cope; and the swing when it comes is sudden and emotional. The new system 'makes converts', and the old one just fades away for lack of followers.

A principle is too basic to be justified or verified in the way that other statements are. So an alternative principle cannot be rationally preferred as more true, more probable, or even more appropriate or respectable. But we do not choose between principles as individuals, but between the systems which are built on them.

The sequence of systems of thought is not a mysterious shadow-play, with each thinker a plaything of the Spirit of his Age. There is a rational succession, and even progress of a sort; though of course the choices made by individuals are never wholly rational, and the factors at work in past periods may now never be completely understood.

54. DO PRINCIPLES DETERMINE THOUGHT?

How far do principles determine a system, and constrain the thinkers who are building it?

In a deductive system the axioms provide the 'matter', creating a field of possible theorems, viz. the set of all the consequences which do flow from them. The rules of inference control the 'form', setting out permitted moves. Individual theorists then try out sequences of moves, each sequence selecting one set of possible theorems arranged in one particular way. Neither axioms nor rules of inference require that any particular system should be built. You need bricks and mortar in order to build a house, but they do not determine what sort and shape of house you build.

XI.54 Do principles determine thought?

In non-deductive systems the rules of inference are mostly more relaxed; and the set of starting-points is in practice much wider and less definite. The builder's freedom is all the greater, here.

Looking backward, the relation of presupposition seems as strict and 'determinative' as implication. For John's children all to be in bed it is first required that John have children: required willy-nilly, with no ifs and buts. For an astronomer to develop some theory describing the orbits of planets he must first have a theory whereby those apparently wandering stars do move in regular paths around the sun. But this necessity is all one-way. The fact that planets do orbit the sun does not determine at all what shape those orbits are to take. John's having children does not of itself bring it about that they are in bed.

Presuppositions are suppositions which have to be made before we can proceed in some given way. Adopting them does not in any way make us proceed in that or any other way, it only makes it possible. By the same token, principles of method or of inference do not determine what inference we shall make. To take another analogy, the principles taken for granted in a scheme of thought may lead us to look in certain directions, but do not settle what we shall see when we look that way. So cultural relativism - the view that we all willy-nilly look at the world through the spectacles provided by our culture and our age - does not imply any sort of determinism. Whatever the spectacles, we are free to look - and see.

The question remains, how far we are free to change our spectacles. Of course we shall not even try, until we realize that we are wearing them. The thinker who leads an unexamined life is bound by his present set of principles, inherited or acquired. But suppose we become aware of what we presuppose, can we evaluate those presuppositions in some way, and deliberately exchange them for another set?

On Collingwood's view, presuppositions which are absolute answer no questions, so are neither true nor false. Lacking logical properties, they are not a matter for rational choice; each of us must manage with the set he has. Philosophers can

XI.54 Do principles determine thought?

however discover by analysis what is absolutely presupposed in the science of some given age, and philosophical historians can trace the stages by which one set of presuppositions comes to be replaced by another set: though reasons can hardly be given, as the whole process is irrational (48n). Collingwood does not give very convincing reasons for this view: perhaps he accepted this form of cultural relativism first on other grounds, and later noticed that it could be made to fit his question-and-answer theory of science.

There are indeed 'absolute presuppositions' in any ordered scheme of thought, and of two quite different sorts. There are existential or referential assumptions: that planets exist, that there is a man called John. For theories must have entities to be about, or else fail for emptiness. A referential assumption may be taken as ultimate if we can't see that it has any further assumptions of its own, or if we see no point in carrying our analysis beyond this one (cp Toulmin 1972).

Then there are principles: rules of method or of inference. It is by these that we generate whole tracts of systematic thought. We regard such a rule as more 'basic', the more we would have to throw away if it were lost. A principle is fundamental to some whole system if discarding it means destroying that system as a whole. The fundamental character of a principle is thus decided by reference to the thought-system, the 'science' based on it, and not by reference to the scientists using it, or to the age in which they live.

Fundamental principles and existential assumptions, once discovered, are both open to revision after taking thought, but not in the same way. Existential assumptions are revised in a straightforward and piecemeal way, by slightly changing our theories, and amending our definitions of the corresponding terms. Fundamental principles are replaced, rather than revised. A new system, employing the new principle, grows up beside the old. Then people change over, accepting the new principle because the system it informs appears to them a better one (cp Palmer 1977, Rosenberg 1977b).

55. THE WORK OF DEFINITION

How do the existential assumptions involved in terms like 'orbit', 'witchcraft', 'vacuum' get revised? Before answering, we must first say briefly where terms come from, and come to be defined.

In any natural language, not yet re-furbished by philosophers, we find both words and terms. Some items are precisely defined, as 'technical terms' of this or that specialty: Labrador, Lieutenant, Legatee. Others cover a wider and less definite area, and in some we can distinguish a whole series of 'senses', related in a variety of ways, and with no one factor common to them all.

These vague, untidy, straggling words come first, and neat meticulous terms a long time afterwards. The terms are in fact created, by definition, and mostly from existing words, though now and then a new word is made up (gas, stunt). In other cases a new term is made up out of simpler elements previously defined (reflation, polymer).

In some largely formal systems, such as logic and geometry, the entire technical vocabulary is built up in this way from a very few initial words from common life. The terms in such systems can all be traced back to these few 'primitives', just as the theorems must all be derived from a short list of initial axioms. This fundamentalist approach is reflected in the accounts usually given of definition or 'introduction' of terms (see above #35). But for everyday technical purposes such purism is quite impractical. In practice, a term is created by taking a word or phrase which is near the desired meaning, and then stipulating the precise limits of the technical connotation we desire it to bear: as who should say "for the rest of this book 'marginal propensity to save' shall mean precisely and only X and Y and Z, and let the reader beware of understanding anything else or more by it!" Such appropriated and precisely delimited symbols, if they find favour and use, may then be adopted in perpetuity by that learned community, sometimes even with formal ceremony at a conference on terminology (cp Field 1932).

XI.55 The work of definition

Definition is free, of course: 'free-but', as other human actions are. The new meaning stipulated for a term will in practice have to keep quite near to common usage, to gain the advantage of familiarity; and it should consort with other terms previously defined. Which looks quite easy, until you try. Most definers lose patience long before they have got the complications sorted out.

It is no doubt easy to propound a single and startling re-definition, thus showing definition to be fully free. "There's glory for you", said Humpty Dumpty, explaining that by glory he meant 'a nice knock-down argument'. But Humpty Dumpty could not have kept up a conversation on theology, for he would not know which of his re-defined terms would consort with any other one. When we come to relational terms, and metaphysical, the going is more difficult: it takes a Spinoza or a Hegel to work out a system of thought of even moderate consistency, while assigning new meaning to all the fundamental terms.

In the past, writers who thought they could improve one or another such system would do so directly, publishing the results of their tinkering as a new system of their own. The same tinkering is nowadays described as linguistic analysis or conceptual research, and presented as a set of discoveries about the 'concept' of democracy, or of mental agency, etc (cp Haas 1972).

Let us call such tinkering 'the work of definition'; and ask what value it may have. It is not just a personal and arbitrary play with words, as Humpty Dumpty's was. It is done in a social context, against a background of many other accepted concepts, more or less defined, with which this one now under revision is going to have to mesh. It is worth doing, in moderation, because it traces out the links between the concepts that we have, as well as suggesting slightly different ones which, if adopted, might make the world look somewhat different. Now, is that new vision of the world better or cleverer, more comprehensive or more comforting? If so, that is the real point and profit of this game of words and terms. Who would go on playing it, unless they found it so?

XI.55 The work of definition

Definition and presupposition are two sides of one coin. By definition we fix an equivalence between the terms defined and several other words and terms. By 'presupposes' we relate one of these to the term defined, as its ingredient. So any discussion of definitions can also be carried on by reference to presupposition and ingredience (cp Rynin 1964).

Collingwood has a picture of a communal set of basic non-propositions, not believed and therefore unrevisable, yet subject to gradual modification which the conceptual historian can record. This picture is partly true of terms. Languages do change, for various reasons - though deliberate revision by the language-users is not a major one. Each change creates new 'strains', putting a different gloss on many terms, until some are finally rendered obsolete. The usual remedy is to make new terms. Some specialties can be found sporting several alternative terminologies, each partly fossilized (e.g. philosophy). Another solution is to propose re-definitions, trying to keep the old term to its original meaning by explaining it in different words (e.g. theology).

Language changes, and our definitions must change with it, if our concepts are to stay the same: you have to run quite fast linguistically, to stay in the same place conceptually. For if the terms used in a definition change their meaning, then so will the term they define, unless we re-define to stay the same.

It can also happen that our concepts change. Here we go on using old words to express quite new ideas, usually because we would like to 'keep the goodwill of the business'. Presumably it is better if we do this knowingly, and better not to change too many things at once (cp Kripke 135f).

56. REVISING BASIC ASSUMPTIONS

An assumption which underlies a whole system of thought cannot be revised within that system. Replace it by another assumption, and a whole new system is required. At first, it seems in conflict with everything we know: but gradually a new system grows up beside the old and people begin to move across. The move can take on the dramatic character

XI.56 Revising basic assumptions

of a religious conversion: for the mover, everything has to change at once.

The assumption replaced, being fundamental to the system it figures in, cannot be judged true or false within that system: for it helps provide the basis and standard by which the rest of the system is to be verified. So the new assumption cannot be preferred to the old as 'nearer to the truth'. But the new system can be rationally preferred to the old, and it is quite rational to prefer the new assumption just because the system it makes possible is a better one.

In what way better? A system which explains more, or explains the same things more simply, with fewer exceptions or special hypotheses, may be preferred on these 'object-related grounds. There are also structural bases for comparison; one system may be simpler in overall structure, or show less internal conflict, or require fewer independent axioms or primitive ideas. These various dimensions of systematic preference are a commonplace in the philosophy of science. Now if one system can be rationally preferred to another, that gives a reason why an assumption fundamental to the latter system should be dropped in favour of one basic to the system we prefer (cp Mintek 1977).

Self-conscious system-choice is of course a fairly late development; indeed we have hardly reached it yet. At earlier stages the same rational factors may influence preference, but those doing the preferring have a wrong picture, or no picture at all, of what is going on.

When people do not realize that they are assuming anything, in their system of ideas, they find it quite upsetting to confront another system built on assumptions equally hidden but rather different. The opposing system strikes them as unintelligible or contradictory. This feeling of radical otherness is instanced daily in the clash of religious and dogmatic ideologies. It can also be seen in early accounts of magic as misdirected science, and indeed in reactions to scientific procedures by those accustomed to forms of thought we label 'superstitious' or 'magical'.

XI.56 Revising basic assumptions

At a later stage system-change gets assimilated to theory-change: evidence is demanded for the new assumptions, and it cannot be produced. The change may then be rejected as irrational, or commended as a 'leap of faith', the necessary unreason being brazened out as a virtue and even generalized to a theory of cultural determinism or relativity. A time should however come in each culture when the thinkers involved in such a change realize what is happening to them. Recognizing that assumptions are made, not discovered, and that their input is structural, not informational, the theorists involved should take their sea-changes more calmly, and continue the dialogue with those on 'the other side'(cp Sinclair 23f).

When such revolutionary changes do take place the thinker still has to 'jump' from one system to the next. Knowing that he is jumping, and why, will not tell him which way to jump, though it may make him a more sophisticated jumper, and perhaps a less unhappy one.

57. WHAT TRANSCENDENTAL ARGUMENTS CAN DO

Such revolutionary change is fortunately rare. It occurs only when basic assumptions are revised. Less fundamental revisions can be appraised on their merits, one by one, without bringing the whole house of cards tumbling after them.

How do we tell an assumption is a fundamental one? That should be a simple matter of inspecting the logical structure of that science: e.g. Euclid tells us at the start what are his axioms and his postulates. But very few sciences and thought-systems are sufficiently well-structured for us to read our answer off like that. 'Getting back to first principles' may involve much dispute and prolonged analysis.

Collingwood suggested a psychological sign: scientists are 'ticklish' in their absolute presuppositions - provided they had not been spoilt by talking to philosophers (44; cp above #4). But by writing on this topic, in a way that even scientists can understand, he has helped to dry up the supply of suitable diagnostic frogs. Some better test is now required.

XI.57 What transcendental arguments can do

Transcendental argumentation was meant to provide some justification for such fundamental principles; justification which has turned out to be inevitably circular. But this fact itself may help us to make out which of our theoretic statements are most fundamental, which ones are really 'principles'.

But surely we must know what we are presupposing, at any given stage? In most cases, no. Items taken for granted are thereby set aside, uninspected; especially if one party takes them over, in discussion, from another one. Working out what things are presupposed in a current system of thought requires much abstract reflection and analysis and the theoretical entertaining of alternatives where common sense and received opinion both assure us that there are none to entertain.

How can transcendental arguments assist in this? They are normally put forward only as a last resort. No-one, so far, has tried to justify Boyle's Law by a transcendental inference. For we can test it out within experience, fully expecting that if it does not really hold then sooner or later experimental findings will conflict with it. And there are more basic or wider physical laws, to derive it from. While these normal avenues remain open for justificational research, no-one takes the high transcendental road. And if they did, it would not work; for abandoning a true low-level law would not wreak enough destruction to show that law a condition for our knowing anything at all.

An absolute presupposition cannot be justified, i.e. shown true, by transcendental arguments, since that use of them is circular. It may be shown unavoidable-for-Smith, undeniable for those who hold a certain set of views. Or it can be turned round into a pragmatic argument: a presupposition on which so much is built must surely work! But the fact that we resort at all to transcendental argument, and that some such reasoning can be even plausibly advanced in a given case, does show that the item there defended can claim the status of a basic principle. For only principles are plausibly defensible by means of transcendental inference. Thus an argument which fails to justify some principles as being true may at least serve to establish them as principles (Palmer 1978).

58. PRINCIPLES AND PARADIGMS

This account of the revision of presuppositions has obvious parallels with Kuhn's account of the revising of scientific theories. For him, low-level theories are under constant slight revision or extension in the bread-and-butter research of 'normal science': basic theories or 'paradigms' are revised very rarely, and then with explosive, revolutionary effect.

The effect Kuhn portrays so dramatically is not restricted to science, and it is not irrational. It is not very frequent either, being bothersome, usually avoidable, and difficult to think about.

An existential presupposition can usually be expressed with a denoting phrase, such as 'the planets move in orbits '; and this can be replaced by a statement of theory, with a 'that' in front: "that the so-called wandering stars do move in regular recurring paths". 'John's children' goes over to "that John has children", and even 'John' can be analysed into "at a certain house lives a man who bears this name". Each such existential presupposition can thus be equated with some statement of that theory or system of ideas.

A similar conversion can be applied to whatever is ultimately presupposed. It may be taken completely for granted, in a certain science, that every event must have a cause. Yet we can decide to discuss this very point. To do so, we shall take other things for granted and regard this as a theory or hypothesis. No set of statements is a theory by nature, nor are any of them intrinsically presuppositional. They have these greatnesses thrust upon them: something becomes an assertion, by being asserted; a presupposition, by being presupposed. Whether to say X, or to take X for granted while we are busy saying Y, is a matter for our choice. Assertion and presupposition both bear a systematic character; and what is presupposed in one system of thought it may well be the business of another science to assert. Our choice comes in when we decide to work or think in this system or in that.

178

XI.58 Principles and paradigms

People do not, of course, change systems quite as they take up a new pencil or change their hats. It is enough work for most, to master one system well enough to do useful work in it: one language, one religion, one geometry. Very few can entertain two systems in a given area, let alone compare and assess them, explaining why one should be preferred.

For this reason, among others, systematic change is very gradual. Some changes are merely structural, e.g. if one axiom is demoted to the rank of theorem, and some other theorem promoted in its place. We could thus obtain several systems of Euclidean geometry, different axiomatic arrangements of the same material. In the same way one might devise a 'new' system with one item as axiom which, in the old system, was taken completely for granted.

Where an axiom is actually exchanged for a different one (e.g. the axiom of parallels) a materially new system is generated, though all the other axioms remain the same. And so it might go on, until all have been replaced, as in Neurath's image of a ship rebuilt plank by plank <u>at sea</u>. The process has to be gradual, as you need somewhere to float and live and think and work from in the meantime. A system of thought is not just a set of related propositions external to our minds, to be set down in books and stored in libraries. It is a way of working, which cannot be shed or exchanged all at once, though it is all subject to revision for good reasons, bit by bit.

BIBLIOGRAPHY

BOOKS

On the right is the number of the section where that book is referred to (or to which it is relevant). A letter following indicates a Note. The number of pages is given before the publisher. '+' means 'and others'

ARISTOTLE	Metaphysics (trs. Warrington) 388 Dent 1956	22
W W BARTLEY	The retreat to commitment 223 Chatto + 1964	(56)
L W BECK,ed.	Kant studies today 507 Open Court 1969	(21),48
	Kant's theory of knowledge 217 Reidel 1974	19,48
R J BENTON	Kant's second critique and the problem of transcendental arguments 172 Nijhoff 1977	47
N O BERNSEN	Knowledge 686 Odense 1978	22,50
P BIERI +,eds	Transcendental arguments and science 314 Reidel 1977	(6),47,48 50,54
F H BRADLEY	Appearance and reality 558 Oxford 1893	43

Bibliography - Books

G G BRITTAN	Kant's theory of science 215 Princeton 1978		23
C D BROAD	Kant, an introduction ed Lewy,332 Cambridge 1978		24C
R BUBNER,ed	Zur Zukunft der Transzendentalphilosophie 142 Vandenhoek + 1978		44,47 48
J BUTLER	Dissertation on personal identity 1736		43
L CARROLL	The Penguin complete Lewis Carroll 1165 Penguin 1982		37
P COLE,ed	Radical Pragmatics 328 Academic,NY 1981		15,38D
R G COLLINGWOOD	An essay on metaphysics 364 Oxford 1940		4,15 52,54
D E COOPER	Philosophy and the nature of language 220 Longmans 1973		38D
I M COPI	Introduction to logic 604 Collier Macmillan 1982		18B
R DESCARTES	Collected Works, ed Haldane +		1-13

    I 7,20   Rules   II 26,38,62   Objections
    92,99f   Discourse   115,136f   and
    220f   Principles   167,205f   Replies
    150,159f   Meditations   220,266,282.
    324   Search   127   Letter

A DONAGAN	The later philosophy of R.G.Collingwood 332 Oxford 1962		52
J L EVANS	Knowledge and infallibility 160 Macmillan 1978		39
P T GEACH	Reference and generality 202 Cornell 1962		39
M S GRAM	Kant, ontology and the a priori 194 Northwestern 1968		47

Bibliography - Books

S	HAACK	Deviant logic 191 Cambridge 1974	18,32
C J	HALE	Contemplations moral and divine 1671, cited Rolph, <u>Times</u> 16.8.82	
C L	HAMBLIN	Fallacies 326 Methuen 1970	18B
R	HARRISON	On what there must be 210 Oxford 1974	43
N	HINSKE	Kant's Weg zur Transzendental-philosophie 172 Meiner 1970	49E
D	HUME	A treatise of human nature,I 1738	43
I	KANT	Inaugural Dissertation of 1770 trs Eckoff,101 AMS Press 1970	25
		Prolegomena to any future metaphysics that will be able to present itself as a science (1783) trs Lucas, 155 Manchester 1953	23,27f
		Philosophical Correspondence ed Zweig, 260 Chicago 1967	21
R	KEMPSON	Presupposition and the delimitation of semantics 235 Cambridge 1975	16,38,38D
K L	KETNER	An emendation of R.G.Collingwood's doctrine of absolute presuppositions 41 Texas Tech 1973	52
S	KORNER	Kant 230 Penguin 1955	24
M	KRAUSZ,ed	Critical essays on the philosophy of R.G.Collingwood 357 Oxford 1972	(52)
S	KRIPKE	Naming and necessity 172 Blackwell 1980	55
T S	KUHN	The structure of scientific revolutions 207 Chicago 1970	58

Bibliography - Books

R	LATTA +	The elements of logic 393 Macmillan 1964	42
L	LINSKY	Referring 135 Routledge + 1967	(15)
J	LOCKE	Essay concerning human understanding 1690	36,42
J L	MACKIE	The cement of the universe 340 Oxford 1974	25
J N	MOHANTY +	Essays on Kant's Critique of Pure Reason 285 Oklahoma 1982	46
J S	MILL	A system of logic (1843) 571 Routledge 1905	14A
CWK	MUNDLE	A critique of linguistic philosophy 279 Oxford 1970	17
L	NELSON	Progress and regress in philosophy trs Palmer 256,288 Blackwell 1970,1971	22 48,51
R	OTTO	The idea of the holy trs Harvey, 254 Oxford 1926	40
H	PALMER	The logic of gospel criticism 260 Macmillan 1968	48
		Analogy 186 Macmillan 1973	5,43
H J	PATON	The categorical imperative 283 Hutchinson 1946	45
C S	PEIRCE	Collected papers 392,535 Harvard 1932 or see J BUCHLER,ed The philosophy of Peirce 386 Routledge 1940, pp 27,228f,256,293	4,6
T	PENELHUM +,eds	The first Critique 147 Wadsworth 1969	48
R S	PETERS	Ethics and education 319 Allen + 1966	43
	PLATO	The Republic, trs Cornford 356 Oxford 1941	41

Bibliography - Books

J	REE	Descartes 256 Lane 1974	4
R	ROBINSON	Definition 207 Oxford 1950	(55)
D	ROSS	Foundations of ethics 328 Oxford 1939	43
L	RUBINOFF,ed	Collingwood and the reform of metaphysics 413 Toronto 1970	(52)
A	SINCLAIR	The conditions of knowing 260 Routledge 1951	56
L S	STEBBING	A modern introduction to logic 525 Methuen 1930	36,14A
D	STOVE	Probability and Hume's inductive scepticism 133 Oxford 1973	37
P F	STRAWSON	Introduction to logical theory 266 Methuen 1952	15,47
		Individuals 247 Methuen 1959	43,47
		The bounds of sense 296 Methuen 1966	24
RCS	WALKER	Kant 214 Routledge + 1978	24C
T E	WILKERSON	Kant's Critique of Pure Reason 232 Oxford 1976	24C,47
T C	WILLIAMS	The concept of the categorical imperative 142 Oxford 1968	45
D	WILSON	Presuppositions and non-truth-conditional semantics 161 Academic 1975	38D
L	WITTGENSTEIN	On certainty 90+90 Blackwell 1969	5,17

ARTICLES

On the right is the number of the section where that item is referred to (or to which it is relevant). '+' means 'and others'.

Abbreviations:

    J (ournal of)
    Q (uarterly)
    R (eview of)
    Ph (ilosophy,   ..ical)
    P (roceedings of the) A (ristotelian) S (ociety)

Brief summaries are given. Fuller and more authoritative abstracts may be found in Review of Metaphysics or in Philosophers' Index.

H E ALLISON   Transcendental idealism and
1969   descriptive metaphysics   44
               Kantstudien 60. 216-233
Strawson wants Kant's Deduction without his idealism, so ends up just re-affirming our 'natural' beliefs, not justifying them. 'What our experience requires' might not be quite right.

H E ALLISON   Transcendental affinity - Kant's
1974   answer to Hume   19
               in Beck, 119-127
We might prove things must hang together, even though we cannot see the links.

H E ALLISON   Kant's refutation of realism   (19)
1976   Dialectica 29. 223-253
Kant's 'phenomena' are real things as seen from where we are. All realists don't realize is what they are contributing.

K AMERIKS   Kant's Transcendental Deduction
1978   as a regressive argument   47
               Kantstudien 69. 273-287
The Deduction works back from the fact of knowledge to the items needed for such knowledge to be possible. Transcendental Idealism is one of these.

K AMERIKS   Recent work on Kant's theoretical
1982   philosophy   30
               American Ph Q 19.1-24
Reviews recent understandings of the Transcendental Deduction, and of how noumena were supposed to differ from phenomena.

Bibliography - Articles

I   ANGELELLI On the origins
1972   of Kant's 'transcendental'   49E
         Kantstudien 63.117-122
T-predicates fitted everything, for scholastics: showed some a priori propositions O.K., for Kant. The link may be their explanatory character (cp Hinske).

R E AQUILA   Two kinds of
1976   transcendental argument   45
         Kantstudien 67. 1-19
One from phenomena to their transcendental grounds, one from our knowledge of phenomena to what makes such knowledge possible. Kant's can be read either way, don't quite work in either but seem to if conflated.

R E AQUILA   Personal identity and Kant's
1979   Refutation of Idealism   30
         Kantstudien 70.259-278
T D (B) says a unified consciousness must recognize intuitions as assembled. R of I argues that an actual particular Me needs articulation as to before, after and same time: need Things, for that.

L   AQUIST   Reflections on the logic
1962   of nonsense   33
         Theoria 28.138-157
A three-valued calculus.

J D ATLAS   On presupposing   38D
1978   Mind 87.396-411
'exist' is non-specific, not ambiguous. So is 'not'.

P   BALASUBRAMANIAN The concept of presupposition
1979   Ph D thesis, Madras   37
Presupposition taken as converse of implication; a conclusion presupposes its premisses. This relation is asymmetrical and aliorelative, and has truth-table TTFT. No third value is required.

W H BARNES   Referring to individuals   (17)
1973   P A S 73.167-179
Reference is to something present or remembered, or taken on trust from one who does. Success may not guarantee existence:- 'that accident I nearly had'.

Bibliography - Articles

M BAUM Transcendental proofs 23,47
1977 in Kant's Critique
in Bieri, 3-26
Körner's uniqueness objection tells against Strawson but not Kant, who argues regressively only in Prolegomena (see also Bittner 1977, Cramer 1977).

J BENNETT Analytic transcendental arguments (47)
1977 in Bieri, 45-63
Conceptual analysis can show what the would-be solipsist cannot do without, and this should limit the unthought-of theories he can say he's waiting for. He can't always play the joker "But is it really true?" (cp Patzig 1977, Körner 1977).

R J BENTON Transcendental arguments in
1978 Kant's Groundwork ... 47
J Value Inquiry 12.225-237
A deduction is transcendental if it vindicates a cognitive framework by showing how two faculties work together. Instance regarding (not, proving) Categorical Imperative.

M BERGMANN Presupposition and 33
1981 two-dimensional logic
J Ph Logic 10.27-53
Propriety is not a third value but a second dimension on which statements are assessed. Policies for defining connectives on this 4-value scheme, e.g. make impropriety contagious.

P BIERI Scepticism and how to take it 6
1977 in Bieri, 299-307
Yes, the sceptic must be taken seriously - as a dramatic pose meant to bring out our predicament (cp Stroud 1977b).

G BIRD Kant's transcendental idealism (19)
1982 in G Vesey,ed Idealism past and
present, 71-92
When Kant calls cosmic talk empty he does not mean it's meaningless, only that we can't apply it. T I is not a version of phenomenalism.

R BITTNER Transcendental arguments, (23)
1977 synthetic and analytic
in Bieri, 27-35
No-one consciously synthesizes ideas (cf Baum 1977).

Bibliography - Articles

J M BOYLE   Self-referential inconsistency,   9
1972   inevitable falsity and metaphysical
               argumentation
                    Metaphilosophy 3, 25-42
The inconsistency is factual yet unavoidable: some
things Smith would be in no position to say,if true.

J M BOYLE +   Determinism, freedom and   14
1972   self-referential arguments
                    R Metaphysics 26,3-37
Determinism is false as its being stated conflicts
with what it says. This falsity is necessary but
factual. Such refutation does not beg the question,
is not <u>ad hominem</u>, and differs from <u>reductio</u>
(cp Malcolm 1968).

R BUBNER   Kant, transcendental argument, and
1975   the problem of the Deduction   22
                    R Metaphysics 28.453-467
To discuss or justify some knowledge you need to
know it first ('self-referential'). The Deduction
cannot precede it, as from some higher principle.

R BUBNER   Transcendentalism and protoscience   36
1977   in Bieri, 191-195
'Constructing a protophysics' just by orderly
'introduction' of the basic concepts does not
validate physics; and you'd need the physics first.

B L BUNCH   Presupposition, an alternative   32
1979   approach
                    Notre Dame J Formal Logic 20.341-354
Presupposition is subjunctive, dispositional,
personal, circumstantial, conversational, not just a
logical relation between statements in mid-air (cp
Govier 1972, Post 1968,1972).

W CARL   Comment on Rorty   48
1977   in Bieri, 105-112
Attempt to rule out all alternative conceptual
schemes is feasible. Argument from untranslatability
(Davidson) does not make vindications illegitimate.

C E CATON   Stalnaker on pragmatic   38D
1981   presupposition
                    in Cole, 83-100
Pragmatically presupposed beliefs are indicated as
currently common to speaker and hearer, and quite
strongly held. Semantic variety still needed too.

R M CHISHOLM   What is a transcendental argument?   48
    1978   in Bubner, 19-22
Formulates a transcendental move from noting some present S which requires P to asserting P. To avoid refutation the sceptic-re-P may deny S or else question hypothesis that S requires P.

R M CHISHOLM   The directly evident   10
    1979   in G Pappas Justification and
                    Knowledge, 115-127
Admits things which you do know if you've got (toothache); you refer all these to one have-er, which is the nearest you can get to 'I'.

L J COHEN   Can the conversationalist hypothesis
    1977   be defended?   38D
                    Ph Studies 31.81-90
Difficult cases debilitating Grice's scheme to keep meaning truth-functional by treating wayward 'implicatures' as occasional.

D D COLSON   The transcendental argument   (43)
    1980   against determinism
                    Southern J Ph 20.15-24
'intentional' behaviour-patterns not predictable on causal basis. No regress here (cp Malcolm 1969).

K   CRAMER   A note on transcendental propositions
    1977   in Kant's Critique   47
                    in Bieri, 37-43
These are synthetic, non-empirical, and concern assembling of observations: viz. the Analogies. No others have transcendental proofs.

P   CRAWFORD   Kant's theory of philosophical proof
    1962   Kantstudien 53.257-268   45
Transcendental propositions are unobvious principles basic to but not constitutive of a given science or sector of experience, which proves them by being impossible without.

C E DAVIS   Transcendental arguments   47
    1978   Ph D, Cornell
TAs refute scepticism from conditions needed for understanding terms for stating scepticism with. Some work.

M R DENNING   in Regina v Chief Constable   44
    1981   of Devon and Cornwall,Times 21.10.81
Preventing someone from lawfully carrying out his work must be a breach of the peace.

Bibliography - Articles

K S DONNELLAN   Intuitions and presuppositions   15
   1981   in Cole, 129-142
Strawson manages presupposition-in-the-predicate by appeal to intuition, gets stuck on comparisons. Maybe not all intuitions are explainable.

K ENGELBRETSEN   Suggested truth-tables for a
   1975   sentential logic   33
                    International Logic R 8.225f
equivalence = having same value; rest as Aquist 1962

J L EVANS   Error and the will   3
   1963   Philosophy 38.136-148
You may mistakenly think you know, but not deliberately. More errors would be avoided if notion of intuition given up.

G C FIELD   The place of definition in ethics   55
   1932   P A S 33.79-94; and in Sellars +
                    Studies in philosophy(1965)
Definition initial in geometry, final and summary in zoology. Creative stipulation limited in practice. Ethics starts from moral ideas we have, makes more definite and systematic.

M B FOSTER   Christian theology and
   1935,36   modern science of nature   51
                    Mind 44.439-466; 45.1-27
Natural science involves presuppositions which it cannot justify. Philosophy of nature depends on a theology.

A C GENOVA   Kant's transcendental deduction
   1978   of the moral law   51
                    Kantstudien 69.299-313
Not downwards from like propositions higher up, but works sideways, noting some Variety we have unified and saying how we could. Difference of levels redeems the apparent circularity.

A C GENOVA   Transcendental form   47
   1980   Southwestern J Ph 11.25-24
Exhibit transcendental premisses by 'ostensive' argument alongside from premisses about possible experience. Check axioms thus vindicated by an indirect, apagogic proof (inadequate alone).

A C GENOVA   Kant's notion of transcendental   46
    1982   presupposition in the first Critique
              in Mohanty, 99-126
T = justifying as reliable: TD, via presupposition,
non-circular as only justifies phenomena.

M   GINSBERG The entailment-presupposition
    1972   relationship   32
              Notre Dame J Formal Logic 13.511-515
If A entails B, falsity of B requires <u>untruth</u> of A,
thus allowing for reference-failure. Presupposition
thus a species of entailment (cp Stahl 1982).

G di GIOVANNI Paragraphs 20 & 26 of the
    1980   Transcendental Deduction   (26)
              Idealistic Studies 10.131-145
(i) reflective unity particularized in categories is
needed for all thought; (ii) spatio-temporal objects
form system suitable to think about(cp Henrich 1969).

A   GOLDMAN   Can a priori arguments
    1974   refute the sceptic?   42
              Dialogue (Canada) 13.105-109
No, as an extra, question-begging premiss required.
At most they may establish conceptual priority.

T   GOVIER   Presuppositions, conditions
    1972   and consequences   (32)
              Canadian J Ph 1.443-456
Logical properties of presupposition relation;
several sorts, various reasons for priority.

T   GOVIER   Is 'there are external objects'
    1978   an empirical proposition?   50
              Canadian J Ph 7.305-321
Not if provable by a super-transcendental argument
from self-verifying premisses. Any offers?

M S GRAM   Transcendental arguments   47
    1971   Nous 5.15-26
Epistemic premiss, disproved by indirect reasoning.
Incompetent(cp Hintikka 1972, Leaman 1977).

M S GRAM   Must transcendental arguments
    1974   be spurious?   47
              Kantstudien 65.304-317
Non-circular T argument needs epistemic premiss
about things-as-experienced. This, if adequate, too
subjective. Categories of human experiencing not
deducible from 'experience' (cp Hintikka 1972).

Bibliography - Articles

M S GRAM   Must we re-visit
1977   transcendental arguments?   47
            Ph Studies   31.235-247
If special, due to premisses. Interprets B 817 'ostensive not apagogical', B 765 'principle not theorem'(cp Rosenberg 1975).

M S GRAM   Do transcendental arguments
1978   have a future?   47
            in Bubner, 23-56
Kant's sketch and four reconstructions of it all fall down. His actual arguments are important but do not form a class.

M S GRAM   Transcendental arguments,
1979   a meta-critique   47
            Kantstudien   70.508-513
Start with objects-as-experienced, not categorized. Attempts to show categories do apply will either be circular or lead to a regress (cf Leaman 1977).

H P GRICE   The causal theory of perception   38D
1961   P A S Supplement 35.126-132
Suggestions carried, some unavoidably, by what we say (summaries in Kempson, Wilson; cp Cohen 1977, Sadock 1981).

H P GRICE   Logic and conversation   38D
1975   in P Cole +,ed <u>Syntax and
            Semantics 3</u>, 43-58
Normal social conventions presume conversers informative, helpful, truthful; but these can be flouted, for special effect.

P GRICE   Presupposition and
1981   conversational implicature   38D
            in Cole (<u>Pragmatics</u>) 183-198
For decent conversers, remarks about King of France suggest there is one. Not all presuppositions can be so explained, e.g. 'regret'.

H P GRICE + In defence of a dogma   43
1956   Ph R 65.141-158
We may learn to use a distinction we cannot yet define. It is sometimes necessary and even desirable to use terms related to X, in defining X.

A P GRIFFITHS Presuppositions   38
1955   Analysis 16.41-45
Most arguments have holes in but difficult to plug them all; doubting is wrecked by certain doubts.

A P GRIFFITHS Justifying moral principles   43
    1958   P A S 58.103-124
Questioning whether a certain moral principle is
correct involves moral principles, so none can
question all of them. Principle that everyone
counts must be basic.

A P GRIFFITHS Ultimate moral principles   43
    1967   in P Edwards,ed Encyclopaedia
                   of Philosophy VIII.177-182
If anything is to be shown right some moral
principle must be ultimate; e.g. a reason for Smith
is a reason for Jones, if Jones' interests count
then so do Smith's, Jones must be left free to
assess Smith's arguments.

A P GRIFFITHS Transcendental arguments   43,48
    1969   P A S Supplement 43.165-180
May show P must be true for use of language-items S
to be successful, can't also show it is so. Works
on S-user: don't you go denying P!

P   GUYER   Kant's tactics in the
    1982   Transcendental Deduction   31
                   in Mohanty, 157-200
Do TDs assume some synthetic a priori statements, to
justify others? Do they appeal to experience of
thinkers' objects or of independent ones? Three of
these TDs fail, fourth only hinted at and may prove
something different.

W   HAAS   Meanings and rules   55
    1973   P A S 73.135-155
A definition turns a linguistic tendency into a
departmental rule. Not all nonsense can be ruled
out by rules; we can't have rules for everything.

P   HACKER   Are transcendental arguments   48
    1972   a version of verificationism?
                   American Ph Q 9.78-85
Sceptic says objects unreliably inferred from sense-
experience; but not inferred. Inference, doubt and
TD in place when justifying them (cp Stroud 1968).

R M HARE   Plato and the mathematicians   15
    1971   in Essays on philosophical
                   method, 80-97
Hypotheses are things taken for granted in a proof;
e.g. a circle. What would it mean for this
presupposition to be false?

Bibliography - Articles

J HARRISON If I know, I cannot be wrong 39
 1979 P A S 79.137-150
Smith knows p iff he correctly believes p and is well placed to get it right; so 'can't' be wrong.

R HARRISON The only possible morality 43
 1976 P A S Supplement 50.21-42
Reasonable moral judgments require reasons, in a system; defining them as altruistic is just blinkering our vision to what we prefer to see.

R HARRISON Transcendental arguments
 1982 and idealism 47
  Ph Supplement, 211-224
TAs work on a world accessible to mind, a man-made one is not required. Access pays, so our concepts do evolve.

D HENRICH The proof-structure of Kant's 26
 1969 Transcendental Deduction
  R Metaphysics 22.640-659;
  and in Walker,ed 66-81
Two-step, showing can have knowledge within experience, can't beyond. B version better. (cp Giovanni 1980, Robinson 1978, Wetlaufer 1975)

D HENRICH Comment on Rorty 48
 1977 in Bieri, 113-120
Kant not defending one conceptual framework against others. Showing others no better does not show our is good.

L M HINMAN The case for <u>ad hominem</u> arguments 18B
 1982 Australasian J Ph 60.338-345
Opponent's failings, or sources, are relevant if we took his word for the premisses. Inconsistency is always relevant. TAs point out inconsistencies with beliefs everyone must hold.

J HINTIKKA <u>Cogito ergo sum</u>: 12
 1962 Inference or performance?
  Ph R 71.3-32; and in
  W Doney,ed <u>Descartes</u>(1967)
As inference, begs question; as assertion, supplies instance to verify itself.

J   HINTIKKA   Kant's "new method of thought"
    1965   and his theory of mathematics   (21)
               Ajatus 27.37-47
An Intuition is anything standing for an individual.
Geometrical theorems are proved from instances,
which will surely be typical if the mathematical
aspects of the diagram are contributed by us.

J   HINTIKKA   On Kant's notion of Intuition   21
    1969a   in Penelhum, 38-53
Intuitus was direct and particular, not perceptual.
Kant applies to sense-perception and to our
senseless acquaintance with Space and Time.

J   HINTIKKA   Kant on the mathematical method   (21)
    1969b   in Beck, 117-140
Intuition is of individuals or instances.
Construction is a proof-step: 'Let ABC be ...'

J   HINTIKKA   Transcendental arguments,
    1972   genuine and spurious   47
                    Nous 6.274-281
Certain conceptual practices work. What they
presuppose must be true. This is a TA, Kant's
Refutation of Idealism is not (cp Gram Ontology).

J   HINTIKKA   Quantifiers, language-games and
    1973   transcendental arguments   22
                    in Logic, Language-games and
                    information, 98-122
Science as a contest with Nature: try formula, seek
individuals to fit . Kant's 'construction' = have
idea, seek object: works if contributed by me.

R P HORSTMANN Conceptual schemes, justification
    1977   and consistency   (54)
                    in Bieri, 263-269
Conceptual scheme can be justified by showing why
it produces correct or satisfying results. That it
does, is not enough (cp Rosenberg 1977b).

R P HORSTMANN The Metaphysical Deduction in Kant's
    1981   Critique of Pure Reason   26
                    Ph Forum 13.32-47
The ways of unifying deployed in judgments must have
been used first in making Things. Kant thus shows
some concepts constituent in objects (MD), then how
they make knowledge-of-objects possible(TD).

Bibliography - Articles

I L HUMBERSTONE + Two systems of   33
　　1977　　　　　presupposition logic
　　　　　　　Notre Dame J Formal Logic 18.321-339
Presupposition defined in axiomatic three-valued system, using 'strict' validity (cp Woodruff 1970, Engelbretsen 1975).

M G KALIN   What makes an argument
　　1977   transcendental?   47
　　　　　　　Idealistic Studies 7.172-184
Argument to what the experience we do have does presuppose is not _logically_ peculiar. Taking perceptions to need assembling, Kant has just the tackle for the job.

J   KEKES   Metaphysic and rationality   (54)
　　1972   　　Idealistic Studies 2.133-150
Standards for assessing theories are independent but appraisable. Ultimate commitments are various: regulative, categorial, ontological.

D   KOLB   Ontological priorities   42
　　1975   　　Metaphilosophy 5.238-258
i.e. dependence-for-descriptive-purposes: order of real dependence may be different (cp Goldman 1974).

S   KORNER   Transcendental tendencies
　　1966a   in recent philosophy   48
　　　　　　　J Ph 63.551-560
Successful TD would show ours the only way to differentiate objects and attributes. Impossible.

S   KORNER   On the Kantian foundations
　　1966b   of science and mathematics   48
　　　　　　　Kantstudien 57.463-473;
　　　　　　　and in Penelhum, 97-108
We do need some deniable but non-observational regulating principles, when constructing theories. We may make out how our principles work, but can't make sure no others would.

S   KORNER   The impossibility of
　　1967   transcendental deductions   48
　　　　　　　Monist 51.317-331
　　　　　　　and in Beck (1969)
We can see how our way of thinking maps a world, not that it's the only way, or world (cp Schaper 1974).

Bibliography - Articles

S KORNER   On Bennett's 'analytic
1977   transcendental arguments'   47
          in Bieri, 65-69
These only reach inter-subjectivity, then leap to objectivity claiming everything nonsense otherwise.

S KORNER   Uber ontologische Notwendigkeit und die
1978   Begründung ontologischer Principien   48
          in Bubner, 1-18
TD that we must think the way we do, outdated by discovery of other ways, e.g. non-Euclidean geometry. Try again, to isolate concepts basic for our set.

M KRAUSZ   The logic of absolute
1972   presuppositions   (52)
          in Krausz, 222-240
Queries on 'logical efficacy'. Finds further presuppositions for those thought absolute.

O LEAMAN   Transcendental arguments:
1977   Gram's objections   47
          Kantstudien 68.468-477
Kant starts from objects-experienced; notion of Object, derivative. Refutation of Idealism is indirect; such can only show conceptual priority.

O LEAMAN   Transcendental reasoning   47
1980   Ph D, Cambridge
Valid in form, cannot prove existence. Do not discard T Idealism. Regress of justifications takes us back to worth-knowing facts about ourselves.

D S LEE   Distinguishing presupposition   (33)
1972   in epistemology
          Tulane Studies in Ph, 21.85-100
Maps out inference by presupposition to underlying or justifying beliefs.

J E LLEWELYN   Collingwood's doctrine of
1961   absolute presuppositions   (52)
          Ph Q 11.49-60
Irrelevant whether change is made consciously. 'Strain' due to a logical relation, inconsistency.

A C LLOYD   How concepts contain beliefs   16
1958   P A S 58.289-304
Several ways. Some imply beliefs about institutions. That some concepts belief-free, unproven.

Bibliography - Articles

```
J L MACKIE      Proof                              24
     1966            P A S Supplement   40.23-38
```
A system of anaytic theorems may <u>happen</u> to fit certain facts of experience (e.g. geometry).

```
N  MALCOLM    The conceivability of mechanism      43
     1968           Ph R   77.45-72
```
Machines can't assert, so only non-machines can assert mechanism (cp Colson 1980).

```
M  MEYER      Why did Kant write two versions of
     1981          the TD of the categories?       29
                  Synthese   47.357-383
```
TD to show objective knowledge resulting from work of subjective faculties. In A, object a construct, in B just what's given. Resulting variations in meaning and argument systematic, not patchwork.

```
H  MEYNELL    Transcendental psychology         14,47
     1980           Heythrop J  21.153-167
```
A possible science, based on undeniables.

```
S J MINTEK    Rationality and
     1977         absolute presuppositions          56
                  Ph D Washington
```
Belief-system rational if all held <u>subject</u> to revision (cp Bartley <u>Retreat</u>,Watkins 1969).

```
G H MOULDS    Absolute values rediscovered         44
     1972          J Value Inquiry  6.200-212
```
To avoid Absolute Relativism (nothing is so for all) try Linguistic Absolutism (what discussing anything must presuppose).

```
C M MYERS     Circular Explication                 43
     1978          Metaphilosophy  9.1-13
```
An analysis employing the term being analysed need not be viciously circular.

```
G H NEHRLICH  Presupposition and entailment        32
     1965          American Ph Q  2.33-42
```
Are improper remarks statements? Then what is presupposed must also be entailed.

```
B E OGUAH     Transcendental arguments and
     1980          mathematical intuition           20
                  Kantstudien  71.33-46
```
Kant's argument that Space no concept fails. Not shown Geometry synthetic a priori; role of intuition dubious.

H   PALMER   To reduce and to locate   43,53
    1966   Listener 605-6,647-9
Getting rid of God-talk is different from deciding
where it belongs.

H   PALMER   Understanding first   5,43
    1968   Theology 71.107-113
Critique of view that only believers can understand
statements of (religious) belief (cf Phillips 1968).

H   PALMER   Must clocks be material?   30
    1972   Ratio 14.36-44
George's torrent of ideas might include a recurrent
tick by which he learns to time them all; thus
refuting Kant's Refutation of Idealism.

H   PALMER   Interpretive concepts in life
    1977   and history   54
                J Madras U 49.2, 1-11
Historians use concepts they cannot justify but can
commend as making better sense of their evidence.

H   PALMER   Recurring questions and autonomy 57
    1978   Reason Papers,Winter 83-87
Hume's question about induction is 'recurring'. Such
may show the area questioned to be fundamental and
autonomous.

H   PALMER   Are recurring questions serious? 4
    1981a   in Proceedings of C S Pierce
                   Bicentennial International
                   Congress,Texas Tech
Recurring questions and very general doubts which
have no place in everyday life may still be of
service in philosophy.

H   PALMER   Do circular arguments
    1981b   beg the question?   48
                Ph 56.391-398
Circularity is a formal fallacy, question-begging a
misdemeanour of debate, disguising immediate
inference as mediate by adding redundant premisses.

H   PALMER   The Cogito is semi-circular   16
    1981   International Logic R 12.5-15
Conclusion needed for establishing its premisses.
Even if sound it would be language-relative.

Bibliography - Articles

H   PALMER   Revisionary Ifs   38
    1982   Erkenntnis 17.249-261
An 'if per impossibile' licenses cancellation of one
of the preceding premisses, to restore consistency.
Needed only in speech, as taken in bit by bit.

H   PALMER   The transcendental fallacy   19f
    1983   Kantstudien 74.387-404
Presumptive circularity diagnosed in first Critique.

G   PATZIG   Comment on Bennett   47
    1977   in Bieri, 71-75
Transcendental arguments justify concepts and so
restrict their application: the post-revolution
currency is both de-valued and re-established.

D Z PHILLIPS Religious belief and
    1968   philosophical enquiry   43
                   Theology 71.114-117
To distinguish domains of discourse, look and see.
They may overlap (cf Palmer 1968).

H   PILOT   Comment on Rosenberg   (54)
    1977   in Bieri, 271-275
No good just justifying afterwards. Justify
categories as what sceptic can't be heard to deny.

L   POMPA   The incoherence of
    1984   the Cartesian Cogito   10
                   Inquiry 27.3-21
Need to prove Cogito without assuming thinker.
Seems-to-me sentences do this, but aren't statements.

J F POST   An analysis of presupposing   (32)
    1968   Southern J Ph 6.67-71
'presuppose' lacks imperative, performative, takes
personal subject, can be reflexive (see also Ph D
Berkeley 1968)

J F POST   Referential presupposition   (32)
    1972   Australasian J Ph 50.160-167
Logical properties complex, semantic definition
unsatisfactory.

C G PRADO   Rorty's pragmatism   (48f)
    1983   Dialogue 22.441-450
Pragmatism (i)Upper Case - one more philosophy,
(ii) Lower Case - critique of all philosophies,
= don't you dare classify me.

WVO QUINE   Two dogmas of empiricism   43
   1951   Ph R   60.20-43
Accounts of 'analytic' in terms of 'definition',
'synonym','semantic rule' fail for circularity
(cp Grice + 1956).

N   RESCHER   On the logic of presupposition   34
     1961   Ph and Phenom.Research 21.521-527
Propositional, property, inferential,semantic sorts.

H   ROBINSON   A reconstruction of Kant's
     1978   'transcendental'   (26)
                  Ph D SUNY
Rules for dictionary-listing could well generate
T-propositions. Kant's Aesthetic and Deduction work
like this (cp Henrich 1969).

R   ROBINSON   Analysis in Greek geometry   23
     1936   Mind 45.464-473
To prove A seek its consequences, find one true,
work back. Works provided links all 'iff'.
Reductio ad absurdum is a special case of this.

R   RORTY   Verificationism and
     1971   transcendental arguments   48
                  Nous 5.3-14
Can't show alternative concepts parasitic on ours
till got some (cf Stroud 1968).

R   RORTY   Transcendental arguments,
     1977   self-reference and pragmatism   48,50
                  in Bieri, 77-103
TAs need not be anti-sceptical, do involve 'self-
reference' (cp Bubner 1975). Notion of alternative
conceptual schemes incoherent so why justify ours?

R   RORTY   Epistemological behaviorism and the
     1978   de-transcendentalization of
                  analytical philosophy   44
                  in Bubner, 115-142
Conceptual analysis grades culture-areas for
certainty, transcendentally. EB does this better.

J F ROSENBERG Transcendental arguments revisited 48
     1975   J Ph 72.611-623
Kant's are not the only a priori concepts. Move to
new set just if do same job better (cp Stroud 1977).

J F ROSENBERG Reply to Stroud   (48)
     1977a   Ph Studies 31.117-121
TAs just embed concepts in a working scheme.

Bibliography - Articles

J F ROSENBERG Transcendental arguments and
   1977b   pragmatic epistemology   54
              in Bieri, 245-262
New conceptual scheme needs to make more sense of world for us discursive apperceptive synthesizers. Pragmatism has room for this(cp Pilot 1977).

J B ROSSER + Many-valued logics   (32)
   1967   in Copi + Contemporary readings
            in logical theory, 325-341
Dialogue on point if any of non-classical logic.

B   RUSSELL   On denoting   (15)
   1905   Mind 14.479-493
Referents not needed for non-entities, analyse as conjunction to make existential claim explicit.

D   RYNIN   Donagan on Collingwood   55
   1965   R Metaphysics 18.301-333
What Collingwood says does fit definitions.

J M SADOCK   Almost   (38D)
   1981   in Cole, 257-271
'Sam almost died' doesn't imply or presuppose but conversationally implicates he didn't quite.

E   SCHAPER   Are transcendental deductions
   1974   impossible?   48
              in Beck, 3-11
Can't show our concepts best by comparing with experience, might show alternative sets reduce to ours (cp Kantstudien 1972,63.101-116; Körner 1967).

D S SCHWARZ   On pragmatic presupposition   38D
   1977   Linguistics and Ph 1.247-257
Truth-relation, or speaker's assumption?

M   SIMONS   Transcendental deductions revised   43
   1976   Educational Ph and Theory 8.59-67
Principles underlying moral debates are rational not moral (cp Peters Ethics and education).

T J SMILEY   Sense without denotation   33
   1960   Analysis 20.125-135
New two-value connectives, from 3-valued scheme.

G W SMITH   The concepts of the sceptic   44
    1974   Ph 49.149-168
Sceptics preferring not to refer to others should't
say 'I'. Robot-reared fairy-child no exception as
non-solipsist language used in telling tale.

J E SMITH   Radical empiricism   39
    1965   P A S 65.205-218
Relation of comparison not found in experience, as
need basis-for-comparison, which we bring with us.

J   SRZEDNICKI The transcendental impossibility
    1972   of solipsism   48
               Ratio 14.131-143
Solipsism statable only in pluralist language.

G   STAHL   Descriptions et présuppositions
    1982   en logique   (32)
               R Philosophique 172.487-493
Restrict Theory of Descriptions to chosen universe,
allow that items mentioned 'exist'(formally),i.e.
are available for mentioning.

R C STALNAKER Pragmatic presuppositions   38D
    1974   in Munitz + Semantics and
                  Philosophy, 197-213
Define via speakers' intentions, no need for
'logical' relation (cp Caton 1981).

L   STEVENSON Wittgenstein's T D & Kant's P L A 31
    1982   Kantstudien 73.321-337;
                  and in The metaphysics
                  of experience (Oxford)
Against solipsist both urge that judging involves
correction involves comparison involves others.

E   STIFFLER A definition of foundationalism   50
    1984   Metaphilosophy 15.16-25
Some propositions basic to others, accepted without
further evidence; of these, some show things exist.

W P STINE   Transcendental arguments   48
    1972   Metaphilosophy 3.43-52
Verification Principle that TAs 'need' would need
establishing by TA: long short cut(cf Stroud 1968).

J L STIVER   Presupposition and entailment   33
    1975   Southern J Ph 13.485-497
Definition via necessitation yields happier
connectives (cp Van Fraassen 1968).

Bibliography - Articles

P F STRAWSON Ethical intuitionism 43
   1949 Ph 24.23-33; and in Sellars +
                 Studies in Philosophy
Denies feeling X-obliged presupposes X is right.

P F STRAWSON On referring (15)
   1950 Mind 59.320-344; and in Flew
                 Essays in conceptual analysis,II
France having a king is precondition for our describing him, not part of description (cf Russell 1905, Linsky Referring).

B STROUD Transcendental arguments 48
   1968 J Ph 65.241-256;
          also in Penelhum, Walker
Proofs of what we can't-think-without incomplete without some Verification Principle, superfluous with (cp Stine 1972).

B STROUD Transcendental arguments and
   1977a epistemological naturalism (48)
          Ph Studies 31.105-115
"Concept F needed for experience 'F'" should vindicate ghosts. TAs special in conclusion, not form (cp Rosenberg 1975,1977a).

B STROUD The significance of scepticism (6)
   1977b in Bieri, 277-297
Moore, Carnap, Quine don't banish; TA might.

C TAYLOR The validity of
   1979 transcendental arguments 44
         P A S 79.151-165
As embodied agents, must recognize up-down. TAs thus articulate bits needed for view of what we're doing.

J TLUMAK A defective transcendental
   1976 refutation of solipsism 48
         Ratio 18.50-55
Solipsist can think of 'others' without borrowing idea from a pluralist (cp Srzednicki 1972).

S E TOULMIN The problem of relativity 54
   1972 in Krausz, 201-221
Evolving 'absolute presuppositions' should be open to discussion (cp Kekes 1972).

B C VAN FRAASSEN   Singular terms, (33)
    1966   truth-value gaps, and free logic
                J Ph 63.481-494
Allow non-referring names, regard statements containing them as valueless.

B C VAN FRAASSEN   Presupposition, implication
    1968   and self-reference (33)
                J Ph 65.136-152
Define presupposition via necessitation, construct three-valued language in which all explicit, match with ours via 'supervaluations'.

B C VAN FRAASSEN Presuppositions, supervaluations
    1969   and free logic (33)
                in K Lambert,ed The Logical
                way of doing things, 67-91
Build logic with no presuppositions about singular or general terms, by supervaluations (copy truth-values, leave blanks otherwise).

K   WARD   The ascription of experiences   17
    1970   Mind 79.415-420
General predicate presumes range of applications not list of candidates (cp Barnes 1973).

JWN WATKINS   Comprehensively critical rationalism
    1969   Ph 44.57-61 (56)
Being open to criticism about any (not,all) of one's beliefs (cp Bartley Retreat).

A J WATT   Transcendental arguments and
    1975   moral principles   43
                Ph Q 25.40-57
Presuppositions absolute only if unavoidable. Being rational, etc, is nice; but there are egoists about.

J   WETLAUFER On the Transcendental Deduction (26)
    1975   Graduate Faculty Ph J 5.113-131
TD shows categories make experience possible, not how (v.Schematism): so OK-to-use on phenomena (cp Henrich 1969).

T E WILKERSON Transcendental arguments   47
    1970   Ph Q 20.200-212
Enforced by obscure non-logical necessity, reveal linkages in conceptual scheme(cp Wilkerson 199-213).

Bibliography - Articles

L   WOOD   The transcendental method   20
    1962   in Whitney + <u>The heritage of</u>
                    <u>Kant</u>, 3-35
How can anyone say what experience must presuppose?

P W WOODRUFF   Logic and truth-value gaps   (33)
    1970   in Lambert <u>Philosophical</u>
                    <u>problems in logic</u>, 121-142
Alternative tables for connectives in a three-valued system.

H   YARVIN   Language and the <u>Cogito</u>   17
    1977   J Critical <u>Analysis</u> 6.109-118
Principles seeming basic mayn't be compulsory.

E M ZEMACH   Strawson's transcendental deduction 10
    1975   Ph Q 25.114-125
That thoughts need thinkers is what everybody thinks and nobody can prove.

INDEX

Numbers refer to sections of this book, big letters to Notes, Roman figures to chapters.

ad hominem 18B,31
anti-symmetrical 32f
arithmetic 24C
assumption 37,56
astrology 26
atomism 22
authority 8
axioms 22,51

backward 16f,23,VIII,47
Berkeley 41
bivalent 32
Bradley 41
Butler 43

categories VI,48
cause VI
choice 3
circularity III,IV,48
clocks 30
Cogito II,III
Collingwood XI
conditions 16,32f,47
construction 21
contributed V,VI
counting 39
cynic 41

Deduction 23,VI,47
deductive 22,42,54
definition 55
Denning 44
Descartes I,II,III,20
determinism 43
directional 32f
dogmatism 19
doubt I
duty 39
dynamics 22,24C

empirical 20,27
epistemic 11,47

foundations 22,50f
functional 32f,38D

games 5
ganderous 32f
geometry V,VI,42
Gassendi 2,8
Griffiths 44
guiding-thread 25f

207

Index

Harrison 44
Hobbes 13
Hume 19f,41,43
Humpty-Dumpty 17

I 9f
idealism 19,21f,24,30
identity 44
implies 32f,39
indirect 18
infallible 39
ingredient 34f
inside knowledge 10
introduction 35f,42,55
intuition 13,21,25
irreflexive 32f

justification 27,XI

Kant V,VI,40,IX

line-drawing 5
linguistic 17,40,43f,48
Locke 18B,20,36,42

Macbeth 26
Malcolm 43
metaphysics 22,IX
Mill,J S 14A

Otto 40

paradigm 58
paratactic 32
Peirce 4,6
phenomena 19,31
physics 24C,VI
poses 33
pragmatism 26,51f
presupposition IV,VII
--, absolute XI
principles 7,37,42,XI
priority 32,34,42
propriety 16

questioning I

reduction 36,43
reference IV
refutation 12,18,24,30,
                43,47,50
relativism 54
requires 32

scepticism I,50
sciences V,VI,50f
self-reference 9,23
self-verifying 14
soliloquoy 9
space V
spectacles 19,XI
Strawson 44
syllogism 13,14A
synthetic method 23f

terms 40,55
three-valued 32f
Thrasymachus 41
time 22,24C
transcendental X
'transcendental' 45,49E
transitive 32f

undeniable 13f,30
unstated 7

Verification Principle 48

wishful arguing 44
Wittgenstein 5f